Singular People

Ian Breach, Journalist, and his Humanist lives

Introduced and edited by Robert Waterhouse

With a foreword by Chris Mullin

Acknowledgements and dedication

Ian Breach died on January 22 2013: this book has been produced to mark a memorial event for Ian at Loweswater in the North Lakes on May 4 2013. It could not have happened without the cooperation of many people:

First and foremost, Ian himself. During his final weeks we discussed his life and the idea of this book. He dictated recollections of his Manchester childhood. He sorted through Humanist ceremonies he'd taken and kept on file, selecting 12, eight of which form the life stories here;

Ian's wife, Wendy Breach, and his daughter, Emmie Short, both wholehearted supporters of the project;

My wife Jane, who read drafts, drew designs based on William Morris patterns as chapter ends, and gave all-round encouragement;

Ken Brown, who also advised on drafts, as did Martin Woollacott;

Alex Lubrano, who designed and produced the book;

The funeral directors of Cumbria, who were the essential link with the families of the eight lives portrayed here;

The eight families themselves, whose warm response to my many requests reflects their gratitude for the way Ian conducted ceremonies;

The *Guardian*, for permission to reprint Ian's 1974 tribute to Duke Ellington and to reproduce the photograph on page 13;

Roy Saatchi, Howard Perks, Peter Moth and Alex Kirby for their contributions to the section on Ian's tv and radio career;

Patrick Swithenbank for his superb black and white period photography of Ian and Jacky, Emmie and Eric Breach;

Rachel McCormick and Nick Jaspan for help, as ever, with Baquis Press;

Nurses from Tynedale Hospice at Home cared for Ian in his last few weeks; to them, and to the hospice nurses of Cumbria, this book is dedicated

Robert Waterhouse, Manchester, April 2013

Contents

4   **Foreword: The power of will power** by Chris Mullin

6   **My childhood and early life** by Ian Breach

12 **Print journalist, tv presenter, Humanist celebrant** by Robert Waterhouse

28 **Eight lives in a thousand** by Robert Waterhouse

31 **LIFE STORIES** by Ian Breach

31 **Mollie Pearson Abbott**

41 **Julie Broadhurst**

48 **Karen Foulds**

56 **Leslie Halliman**

64 **Deborah Sue Godsey**

71 **Hetty Baron-Thieme**

78 **Charles Bray**

86 **Peter Johnston**

93 **Life has its own meaning**

94 **Tribute to Duke Ellington** by Ian Breach

95 **Picture captions**

96 **Excerpts from Ian's funeral**

The power of will power
Foreword by Chris Mullin

Ian Breach was one of the most talented people I have known. It is often the case that gifted writers - as Ian was - are hopelessly impractical when it comes to mending a fuse or repairing a car, but Ian could turn his hand to anything: joinery, plumbing, motor mechanics, computer repair. You name it, he could do it.

I met Ian and his first wife, Jacky, when I came to live in Sunderland in the autumn of 1985, shortly after having been selected as the Labour candidate for the Sunderland South constituency. At first I lodged with an eccentric doctor further down the same street until Jacky and Ian offered me a place in their basement which I gratefully accepted. Jacky was later to become my secretary.

They lived at 9 Park Place East, one of Sunderland's finest Victorian terraces, in a tree-lined avenue close to the city centre. Although the house still retained many original features, it had seen better days when Jacky and Ian set about restoring it to its Victorian magnificence.

They were both perfectionists and insisted on doing most of the work themselves. On the rare occasions that craftsmen were employed, their work rarely reached Ian's high standards and he usually ended up doing it himself. As a result progress was slow. For all the time that I lived there and for several years beyond, one could not enter the front door without tripping over lengths of timber or copper piping awaiting installation, but the result was a triumph.

Park Place was one of three houses that Ian renovated from top to bottom during the time I knew him. The last, in Hexham, he worked on with Wendy, who he married some years after Jacky's death. Even as he was dying Ian was installing toilets and bathrooms, racing to complete the renovation before his final illness overtook him.

Ian lived dangerously, not always making the best of his considerable talents. There was within him a streak of recklessness which often, to the dismay of those closest to him (who were not usually consulted), resulted in dramatic changes of direction without much thought having been given to the consequences.

I had not been long resident in the Breach household, when Ian suddenly walked out of his job as a presenter with Tyne Tees Television. "Oughtn't you first to have prepared a fallback?" I inquired gingerly. He dismissed the suggestion with a wave of the hand, "Oh, Jacky and I have been over a lot of cliffs together."

His confidence was justified. He set himself up as a freelance and, despite my scepticism, soon had as much work as he could cope with, making environmental programmes for the BBC. Before long he was the BBC's environment correspondent. What better job for the man who, years earlier, had walked out on his job as motoring correspondent of the *Guardian* on the grounds that it was environmentally unsound ?

Unfortunately, his career at the BBC didn't last either. By the mid-1990s Ian's lifelong relationship with alcohol was taking its toll. His life was on a steep downward trajectory. So much so that, at one point, I feared he would end up on the street.

And then, a miracle. In yet another of the dramatic U-turns that marked his life, Ian decided to give up alcohol. After several false starts, an ultimatum from Jacky, and the help of his generous friend John Wilson amongst others, Ian managed to stop drinking once and for all. Not so many years afterwards he did the same with cigarettes, another of his lifelong addictions. It must have required a prodigious effort of will power.

I admire Ian for many reasons, but the effort he put into turning his life around, coming back as he did from a very dark place, was surely his greatest achievement. Once again he re-invented himself, training to officiate at Humanist funerals. Here he was hugely successful. Up until the time he died he was much in demand.

The eight life stories in this book – chosen by Ian from among the 1,000 or so funerals he took – are a testament to his skill and commitment. Astonishingly, he was still conducting other people's funerals even as he was himself dying. "How on earth do you manage?" I asked when I last saw him. He replied "I turn myself into another person for a couple of hours." Again, that amazing will power.

I should say a word about Jacky and Wendy. Ian, who will not always have been an easy person to live with, had the great good fortune to marry two wonderful women. Jacky, who died prematurely in March 1999, was a modest, mild-mannered, highly-intelligent woman of saintly forbearance. If she was looking down in the years when Ian outlived her, she will have been quietly pleased at the way his life turned out. Emmie, their daughter, buoyed up by her own ebullient family, has also coped selflessly with the twists and turns.

And with Wendy, too, Ian once again struck gold. I hope he appreciated his good fortune. Indeed, I know he did.

As for me, I shall remember Ian for the engaging, humane, highly talented if reckless friend that he was – and always with affection.

Chris Mullin was the MP for Sunderland South from 1987 to 2010

My childhood and early life   by Ian Breach

I was born on September 30 1940 in Gatley, Cheshire, where my father, recently recruited to the Army, had uncharacteristically chosen a private nursing home for my confinement. A German blitz was expected (it happened) over central Manchester, and he wanted some measure of safety for my mother Doris.

He was due on basic training at Enniskillen in Northern Ireland, from which he returned briefly and saw me in Manchester before embarking for Madagascar, then India and finally Burma where he served as a Manchester Regiment soldier, eventually a sergeant-clerk in the Fourteenth Army under General Sir Claude Auchinleck (why are we beset by these titles and ranks?).

I next saw my father on November 11 1945, when he arrived back on a troop train in Manchester, having (possibly without irony) sent a telegram to say "Arrived Southampton Expect Home Shortly – Eric."

I have very limited knowledge of what happened to me between the dates of his war service; it amounts to little more than the briefest images. My mother was pregnant with me in a flat somewhere off Slade Lane; father had worked as a clerk in a Manchester textile warehouse but by then was with the CWS as an assistant in their confectionery plant at Reddish.

My mother and father's backgrounds, briefly, were that she was one of nine, living in Openshaw, where my maternal grandfather was a moulder (iron-founder) with a crane-maker; he was later to work for Armstrong Whitworth and was northern secretary for the Iron and Steel branch of the Amalgamated Engineering Union. It was an aspirational family, and all did well in a variety of jobs.

Dad came from a much lower-down-the-social-scale family in Chorltonon-Medlock, later re-housed in Audenshaw, where he was one of five children. His brothers included a fitter at A.V.Roe, an engineer at Linotype and Machinery in Altrincham, and a long-term professional RAF junior officer. Their father was a Manchester tram and then bus driver.

During the war, two of mother's family took my mother and me in as lodgers (though I expect the financial arrangements were loose). We lived for a while in the house owned by her brother Sid and his wife Freda (with boys John and Martin) in Wilmslow; then towards the middle period of the war we moved to live with sister Kit and her husband David (a Tootal employee) in their flat at 147 Mauldeth Road, Fallowfield. It was above a radio and electrical hardware shop, and I remember only that there was a dairy next door, on the corner of Talbot Road, where I badly cut my hands when playing with a broken bottle.

The return of my father proved difficult. He was openly dismissive of and impatient towards a youngster who, it seems, had been spoiled by his mother. We fell out about toys and playthings. It's plain that he was going through the post-war agonies that beset so many returning servicemen. Opportunities that they had lost while away had been exploited by ones who had stayed behind; and – famously – Homes Fit for Heroes was a promise that was patently empty to all but a few, who would have been re-housed anyway.

In 1947 or thereabouts, my parents applied for one local authority house after another but were turned down on grounds of "need", while our wartime lessees – Uncle Dave and Auntie Kit – with no children, got a sizeable new council flat in Burnage. We were about to be made homeless when my Uncle Sid, a clerk and rent collector for a Manchester estate agent, got us a small house on Aden Street in Ardwick.

This was housing soon to be officially condemned in among the classic slums of inner Manchester between Ashton Old Road and Ashton New Road. It had two small bedrooms, no bathroom, one small living room, a scullery kitchen, and a yard with a toilet. It lay adjacent to bombed-out factories along the Dickensian refuse-clad banks of the River Medlock. Surrounding streets were of undiminished squalor, a pub on most corners. A run-down school with ten-foot-high outside walls in Birley Street was my primary school.

My childhood and early life

We lived in Aden Street for about two years, remembered by weekend visits to Grandma Breach's home on Thrapston Avenue in Audenshaw, where they had a bathroom and where my father and I would go for Sunday tea before, in the evening, walking westwards to Openshaw, where my mother would have visited with some of her brothers and maybe sister Kit in the large semi where my Carlile (their surname) grandparents lived. We would take a trolley bus back to Ardwick.

During this period I had begun to take an interest in the industrial backdrop to where we lived. Ardwick was still at the centre of a large network of railway lines in and out of London Road (now Piccadilly) and Victoria stations, of canal routes, towpaths, and roads specifically constructed for the factories and plants that ran outwards towards East Manchester. There were many manufacturing firms, like Gorton Tank where they made engines and rolling stock for railways, makers of cranes and lifting gear like Armstrong Whitworth, and large chemical and steelmaking companies working for the pre-nationalised major suppliers like Lloyds.

Surrounding all of these were countless companies supplying oils, lubricants, solvents, gases, fuel (principally coke from the gas works) and all the other necessities of manufacture. And along the route were more firms, firms into the outside gates of which a young boy on school holidays or on Saturday mornings could stick his head and inspect what was inside.

All along through Bradford (Bradford Manchester) Beswick and Clayton this was the case – from the Mill Street coal mine to the great aniline dyeworks, from Richard Johnson & Nephew (iron-wire manufacturers) to Crossley jet engine works on Pottery Lane. There was industry everywhere.

Around 1949 my uncle found us another house. This was at 16 Eltham Street, Levenshulme, a solid if undistinguished terrace off Stockport Road in a very respectable working class district surrounded by shops and factories. Divided from more upmarket residential districts to the west by the main London railway line, it was industrial home to McVitie's Biscuits, Crossley bus engines, Fairey Engineering (aircraft), and scores of smaller manufacturing outfits.

Further west were Renold Chains and the big machine-tool plants of Wythenshawe. Even though we had moved a very real niche upwards, we were still at a heartland of industry and all that interested me in its products and its processes.

I never developed that at school but, having passed my 11+ exam, rejected the academic potential of Burnage Grammar School by being variously the class clown and wastrel. It wasn't until I went to college in 1956 that I learnt to discover and use the appetite I had developed over the years for the stuff of industry and manufacture.

As in Ardwick, I explored my part of Manchester extensively, wandering into company yards or climbing over railings and fences. I absorbed trade and brand names and could have passed an examination quite early on as to which companies owned which and where some of the early twentieth century international ownership links were to be seen.

I also spent weekends and evenings working in three jobs which made up for formal academic loss. The first and probably most important was that I got a post (as so often by hanging about and chatting) at the Arcadia cinema. This was the "flea pit" of Levenshulme, a long single-storey picture house constructed right up to the edge of the railway line so that fast expresses could be heard quite easily from the front rows.

There were three projectionists, of whom I was one of the two juniors, responsible more or less equally (but without the blame or guilt for anything that went wrong) to the "Chief", a dour Sheffield man who was also responsible for booking the film schedule. It was through his planning that I saw my first foreign movie ("The Wages of Fear") and from whom I learned my love of the precision engineering that went into making a film projector and its associated equipment.

We got to see two "A" and two "B" movies a week and one of varying quality on Sundays. It was also, of course, one of the first non-smoking places I would occupy in my working life (I had already been a smoker since the age of 11 or 12 – given cigarettes by Grandma Breach for running errands).

In between or perhaps at the same time as the job at the Arcadia, I had a job in the local garage where I learned nothing from the owner, who heaped abuse and curses on me but left me alone sufficiently to teach myself about engine maintenance (in those days valves were routinely re-ground and carburetors stripped down to their parts). So a pretty basic car-service course did emerge from this job. Finally, there was a job when I was 15 or so as a baker's van boy, where I got to see bread-making machinery in action.

Chances having been frittered away at school, and with few GCEs passed, I chose a course then on offer around the secondary and grammar schools of industrial Britain: a Board of Trade marine engineering apprenticeship, sponsored by a Merchant Navy fleet owner. In this case it was Shell Tankers, the seagoing arm of what was then the largest oil company in the

My childhood and early life

world. Based in Rotterdam as part of Royal Dutch Shell, they exploited, carried, processed, and sold fuel and refinery oils in a very early and successful global operation using exceptionally large vessels.

I joined one of the first supertankers – the Zenetia – in Europoort Holland and sailed first to Banias in Syria, then to pick up raw crude spirit from Mina al Ahmadi in the Persian Gulf. Later journeys included ones to the Far East, the US east and west coasts and to Columbia and Panama. I gained a lot of engineering knowhow on both steam-turbine and diesel-engine-powered ships, got used to the shift or watch system of working a ship 24 hours a day, and met crew and officers from many other parts and social strata of Britain – including the major naval ports and shipbuilding towns.

In the summer of 1959 I went home on leave with a fellow apprentice who came from Blackpool and, through him, met Barbara Jacqueline Rolaston, a student at Blackpool College of Art. Within a year I had decided to abandon my seagoing career and gave notice to terminate my formal indentures before going to London and joining Jacky in the flat she had set up with a another former student in Hampstead.

She had a job in a couturier's studio in Mayfair; I had no job. But within a week or so was taken on as a technical writer with a West London engineering company CAV, one of the Joseph Lucas group of automotive equipment suppliers (they made "King of the Road" headlights).

After a year or so I moved to work in the West End and found a job as a sales promotion writer with IBM, then recently established as a presence in Britain and a fast-moving force in the world of data processing. A year

or so later, I joined the editorial staff of the Institute of Electrical Engineers, working in Savoy Hill, home of the very first BBC broadcast. It was a tedious but steady job, working with the research submissions of senior IEE staff and consultants around the world of electrical science and electronics.

In May 1964 I began as a subeditor in the features department of the *Guardian* in Cross Street, Manchester. I lacked experience or knowledge of any significant area of the arts or humanities, but it seemed to be accepted that my wider experience elsewhere made up for those omissions. Jacky and I (we had married in 1961) moved from our flat in Primrose Hill to live in Didsbury. The *Guardian* work immediately struck a chord with all that interested me in the paper itself and in the changing approach to design and layout on the features pages.

Print journalist, tv presenter,

There were three distinct phases to Ian Breach's professional life. The first, as a print journalist, from when he started as a technical writer in 1960 to the Penguin Special "Windscale Fallout", published in 1978. The second phase, as a tv and radio reporter and presenter, culminated in late 1994 when the BBC didn't renew his contract. The third, that of a Humanist celebrant, ran from late 1999 to December 2012, only weeks before his death.

Many journalists of his generation moved from print to the broadcast media, whose studios were opening up in the 1970s while newspaper offices atrophied. Few have made a third leap. In Ian's case, the five years or so between professions in the 1990s represented a sequence of crucial life changes.

He was a perfectionist whose impulses propelled his energies. He didn't have much patience for those he felt were less committed. One way or another, he left the employ of the *Guardian*, Tyne Tees Television and the BBC. As a Humanist celebrant he had serious differences with a colleague. And yet, those who were touched by Ian's life force usually benefited. He took life out on himself, not others. **Robert Waterhouse**

A *Guardian* face, up to a point

I first met Ian at the *Guardian*'s Manchester office in May 1964, when we were both young features subeditors. You were what you decided to be at the *Guardian* in those days. As opportunities came your way you swapped roles and departments. Anything seemed possible, though nobody much discussed it.

Ian was a natural writer and sub. Unlike most, he hadn't been to university, but you would never have known. In fact, he was almost pedantic in his desire to find the correct word or phrase, something recognised by Brian Redhead, then northern editor, who asked Ian to revise the *Guardian* style book. I used to tell him that his technical background gave him a huge advantage over Eng Lit types. He wouldn't believe me.

It was the heyday of the *Grauniad*, first editions full of wild typographical errors mainly created by TTS, the far-from-perfect system of simultaneous tele-typesetting used between the London and Manchester offices (new technology in the days of hot metal). The gaffes were nothing much to do with the subs, though we did our best to correct them.

The features department included people like Michael McNay and Derek Malcolm, but Ian held his own. He found a niche looking after the leader

and Humanist celebrant

page, and became letters editor in all but title. It was a job he enjoyed hugely. Chris Dodd, a fellow features sub, remembers him storing letters from crackpots before bundling them up and sending them to Tom Henry (then editor of the *Manchester Evening News*) with cheery notes saying "Any use for you?" and seeing them appear in the *MEN's* 'famous postbag'.

All the same, it was hard not to feel that some faces fitted better than others. One quiet Sunday afternoon, Ian found himself alone in the room with Christopher Driver, who'd recently become London-based features editor. Scanning through newspapers on file, Driver stopped at that day's *Observer* spread where a *Guardian* promotional ad proclaimed: 'For Mahler, Monteverdi and Miles read Cardus, Greenfield and Breach in the *Guardian*'. Without explanation, Driver picked up a phone, tracked down the agency executive at home, and cancelled the ad – all in front of Ian.

Brian Redhead put on a brave front for Manchester, but history was against him and there were many problems. Late one evening, no doubt after a pint or two, Ian and I invaded Redhead's office in the famous corridor: "The airport coaches (they left from Cross Street in those days) advertise 'Read the *Guardian* wherever you fly' but I can't even buy one in Ardwick" Ian chanced. Redhead, with a weary smile, told us to bugger off.

Jazz was big in our lives, and Ian's role as jazz critic gave him the opportunity, at least in theory, to meet the greats. I remember chasing the elusive Thelonious Monk backstage after a fine concert at the Free Trade Hall, Ian calling out despairingly to his leopardskin-coated wife Nellie "Mrs Monk, Mrs Monk..." as they disappeared into the artists' tunnel.

Ian was equally unsuccessful with Miles Davis at Club 43, Manchester's version of Ronnie Scott's. He'd decided to beard his idol during a break between sets and moved in on Miles who, as Ian recalled, was lounging "with his arms around two Manhattan chicks." "Mr Davis, it's Ian Breach of the *Manchester Guardian*, I'd like a word with you please." To which Miles replied, "Go f*** yourself, Mr Breach of the *Manchester Guardian*."

Ian's career: print

Miles remained an idol, and on a happier occasion in the mid-1960s top British musicians Ian Carr, Don Rendell and colleagues were persuaded back to Ian and Jacky's Eccles flat late one week-night for a private concert by the Rendell-Carr Quintet.

Anthony Tucker, the northern features editor who had hired us both, went to London as science correspondent. This was good news for Ian because Phil, as he was known, pushed Ian's case to be offered the new post of technology correspondent, a job he took while still both a Manchester features sub and the paper's national jazz critic. It represented a minor reversal of the Manchester-London drift, but Ian was himself posted to London in 1967. I followed in 1968.

Technology led to motoring. Ian's 1970-72 tenure of the motoring correspondent slot coincided with society's growing concern for the environmental damage caused by 1960s overdevelopment, of which motorways were a large and still-expanding element. Ian took his job seriously, but he couldn't help wondering whether motoring on its own was the correct focus.

He was genuinely shocked by the high-value gifts showered on motoring correspondents reviewing new models, often in lavishly exotic locations. Being Ian, he accepted the gifts but wrote what he honestly thought anyway. His friend Julian Mounter of the *Times* returned gifts unopened, COD, a more principled stand. However, Ian had the final say by exposing the whole tawdry business in a *Sunday Times* colour magazine article.

A bit like the pioneering environmental journalist Kenneth Allsop, Ian loved driving quickly. His custom was to take a road test model out late at night to the bottom end of the M1, then simply see how fast it would go. Hardly an indication of quality, but I recall us both being surprised by the tiny rotary-engined NSU Ro80, which notched up well over 100mph without a murmur. We didn't much care that it was very thirsty and didn't know that it was to be highly unreliable.

Another time, on impulse, we manoeuvred a Steyr-Puch Haflinger all-terrain vehicle he'd been given to test onto rough ground below Alexandra

Palace in North London where Ian tried to overturn it down a hair-raising slope (and prove their publicity wrong). He almost succeeded. Top Gear without the cameras, when Jeremy Clarkson was in short pants.

If these were young men's activities, Ian understood the environmental score and by the time he left the *Guardian* in 1972 (after an unsuccessful attempt to be made transport correspondent) he'd engaged in the battles.

Richard Williams, the *Guardian* columnist and chief sports writer, posted this at the foot of Ian's January 27 2013 *Guardian* online obituary: "I loved reading Ian Breach: a motoring correspondent who detested cars but whose pieces made perfect sense to a car-lover like me. He was one of the writers who formed my idea of what the *Guardian* was about, and made me want to work for the paper."

Atoms for Peace ?

Ian had done a film or two for Allsop's Edition slot, and when after two years' freelancing in London he, Jacky and Emmie moved to Cumbria he couldn't resist bringing the cameras to Milburn, the classic Eden Valley village where he first became a home-owner. By his own assessment it was a poor film, vastly overshot; eventually relations were repaired with villagers, much helped by Jacky who led a successful campaign to save the village school.

Ian was not unaware that most Cumbrian farmers sought financial survival rather than ecological salvation. Wisely, he then left the rural scene alone for the time being: there was something much more important to target just over the hill – Windscale, where British Nuclear Fuels had heady ideas to convert fuel reprocessing technology into an international money-spinning operation.

He'd been brought up on the post-war Atoms for Peace agenda, supportive of nuclear energy as opposed to nuclear weapons, but the more he looked at what British Nuclear Fuels (BNFL, a 100%-owned government subsidiary) was proposing in terms of commercial activity, and at the company's Windscale record, the less he liked it. This was one of those rare stories with international, national and local implications. It was made for Ian.

BNFL was the major employer in jobs-starved West Cumbria. That was enough to ensure local support for a proposal to bring employment both during the construction phase and when THORP (the thermal oxide reprocessing plant) was commissioned. Nationally it would bolster the nuclear power programme, coping with spent waste from reactors around the country. Internationally it was to underline Britain's reputation as a safe provider and at the same time garner lucrative reprocessing contracts from countries such as Germany and Japan.

Ian's own sympathies, in line with people like Walter Patterson at Friends of the Earth, were one thing. But, covering the 100-day Windscale public inquiry conducted by Lord Justice Parker at Whitehaven from June 1977 on a daily/weekly basis for the *Financial Times* and the *New Scientist*, he filed stories in an even-handed way. If he'd done otherwise he'd have been dropped by the *FT*, whose science editor David Fishlock was known to favour nuclear power, and by the *NS*, always heedful of its reputation for impartiality.

The Parker Report, published in March 1978, wholly endorsed BNFL's case and led to Parliament's May 1978 decision to give the project the go-ahead. However, all sorts of questions were left unanswered (including Parker's comprehension of technical issues). It was front page stuff. In the aftermath, Ian was offered a London staff job by the *FT* but decided to stay in Cumbria.

He'd signed a contract to write a Penguin Special. "Windscale Fallout: A Primer for the Age of Nuclear Controversy," published in Autumn 1978, just a few months after the go-ahead, was an object lesson in informed commentary. Ian's conclusion that "the politics of nuclear power and reprocessing will increasingly be those of disillusion, anger, frustration and mistrust" has been born out over the succeeding 35 years.

According to the politics of the era, Parliament was deemed fortunate to be allowed a say on the matter: the vote, which split Labour ranks but was endorsed by most Tories, returned a thumping majority of 144 for the Callaghan minority government; only the Liberals led by David Steel (although part of the Lib-Lab Pact at the time) were united in opposing it.

The energy secretary, one Tony Benn, presented the vote as a sort of victory for open government, while the *Guardian* commented "public opinion, better informed as a result of the Parker inquiry, will not allow its representatives to sanction an unsafe venture."

Friends of the Earth wasn't convinced, Ian quoted in his Postscript. "For all its shortcomings the Windscale inquiry...set standards for the public treatment of nuclear issues that are higher than those reached anywhere else in the world. It is thus all the more tragic that the hasty and erratic judgements of the report on the inquiry did no justice to the proceedings."

Finally commissioned ten years behind schedule in 1997, THORP failed to repay its £1.8 billion set-up investment. Business was hit by stop-start safety concerns and altered nuclear reprocessing markets. In May 2005 the plant was discovered to have been leaking radioactive nitric acid solution (into a second protective jacket) for nine months, for which carelessness it was shut down and the British Nuclear Group fined £500,000. It is scheduled to close definitively in 2018, while the cost of cleaning up the whole Sellafield site, now owned by the Nuclear Decommissioning Authority, has been estimated by the NDA at no less than £72 billion over a 100-year period.

So Sellafield/Windscale, very important to Ian's career (see also page 23) is not about to drop out of the news. As was pointed out by Michael Baron in his letter about Ian's Humanist abilities to the *Guardian* on January 28 2013, Cumbria County Council was that very week to debate whether to allow preliminary work on a huge site for deep burial of nuclear waste. The council voted to join every other in the UK in opposing such a practice. But the plans were backed by many worried about the West Cumbrian economy. Sellafield remains a divisive issue.

Ian's Penguin editor had half-commissioned another Special around the idea of a young person's guide to politics. The editor moved on; the book was never written.

The terrier and the deer

Ian's eyes were already turning to television and his next career move. At 38 he was still youthfully good-looking, sharp, inquisitive and had a deceptively easy manner on camera. He was comfortable both in Cumbria, where he lived, and the North East, where he had family roots.

The 1980s was perhaps the last decade when regional tv companies, and regional outposts of the BBC, attracted ambitious producers, directors and reporters via training schemes and serious programming. For Ian it was natural to look across the Pennines to Newcastle, where both the BBC and ITV had their production centres.

He started as a Cumbria-based reporter for BBC Newcastle, working with people like John Bird and John Mapplebeck at *Look North*. He also made films for the magazine programme Coast to Coast. Bird had originally hired him on the understanding that he cut his hair and stayed away from nuclear power. A 1980 film he fronted for John Metherell, called Mr Bull's Battle, about a week in the struggle of a small firm to stay alive, won a BAFTA.

Commuting from Cumbria, Ian often stayed on week nights with Howard Perks, who edited many of Ian's earliest films, and his wife Jan. Howard writes:

A Primer for the Age of
Nuclear Controversy

Ian Breach

WINDSCALE

FALLOUT

"The BBC North East newsroom was then a hot-house of talent. Sitting next to Ian were fellow reporters Eric Robson (*Gardener's Question Time*), Stuart Pebble (became Editor of *World In Action* then a top dog at ITV), Dianne Nelmes (Director of Daytime ITV and originator of *You've Been Framed!*), Paul Corley (Head of Programmes at Border TV, then GMTV boss) and Roy Saatchi (Head of BBC North West).

"Although a seasoned journalist with a notable reputation, Ian was new to tv but took to it quite naturally. I remember he was once sent by an unsuspecting news editor to cover a big car rally through Cumbria. The story Ian came back with was not the usual blokey gush about fast cars and derring-do rally stages.

"Ian the environmentalist was quite appalled by the event. As the drivers skidded to a halt he asked them if they had considered how much fossil fuel they were burning, what gave them the right to drive on public highways with faulty brake lights, had they considered just how dangerous this was to the spectators and what about their CO2 emissions?

"The piece was transmitted without alteration and then the you-know-what really hit the radiator. Encouragingly, amongst all the predictable complaints from petrol heads, a lot of the feedback was hugely favourable, commending Ian for taking such a fresh and pertinent stance."

Ian then moved to Glasgow where, working with Matt Spicer and Ken Cargill for BBC Scotland on programmes like *Current Account*, he covered the 1981 closure of the Chrysler Linwood car plant following that of the Pressed Steel plant nearby - originally providing bodies for the Hillman Imp. His knowledge of the motor industry and of the UK industrial scene

Ian's career: tv

didn't harm his reputation. He enjoyed Glasgow, and was hoping to persuade BBC bosses to create an environment speciality there, when he was tempted back to the North East.

Reviewing his career only a few weeks before he died, Ian told me the move to Tyne Tees Television in Newcastle, for double the money he was getting with BBC Scotland in Glasgow, was one of the things he most regretted. He felt that he'd been sold down the river by a company primarily keen to secure renewal of its ITV regional franchise in the early 1980s.

He'd been taken on as a heavyweight current affairs presenter. The North East was in turmoil with the closing down of primary industry - coal mines, steel-making plants and shipbuilding yards. Ian was the best-equipped journalist in the region to debate the issues. But, following the franchise renewal, he was left mostly kicking his heels and eventually left. Peter Moth, a former Tyne Tees executive, describes the dilemma from the company's viewpoint:

"If having an ambition to raise the level of your company's current affairs output and hiring an experienced journalist as part of that ambition is a ploy, then I would have to plead guilty when we took on Ian at Tyne Tees. My late colleague Michael Partington would also have to plead guilty as an accessory. We took on Ian because we wanted another journalist with a range of experience which was wider than local newspapers and regional interests...

"When Ian came to us Tyne Tees had ambition. The two Andys, Allan and Wonfor, wanted to see the company punch above its programme weight in ITV, and to a considerable degree they were successful. Ian was part of that success, and we had great hopes of pushing into network current affairs and documentary schedules...

"What Michael and I particularly wanted to break was the schmaltzy soft-centre Plastic Geordie style of journalism which seemed to me to bedevil the region. Ian was at one with us in this ambition, but I don't think we succeeded. The ITV network scene got tougher, and in current affairs it became clear after the new franchises were awarded that the smaller regions were not going to get much of a nose in, and Channel 4 was looking more to independents...

"The result was that in the later period of his time at Tyne Tees Ian quite properly felt frustrated because of the lack of opportunity to enable him to play to his strengths, and his determination not to go down the Plastic Geordie route. By this time I was deeply involved in the company's public

20

affairs and away from programmes, which probably left Ian exposed – he was never good at the politics of management! In that sense he was probably right to regret his move to Tyne Tees, but the rest of us were left regretting his departure."

Leaving Tyne Tees proved all the more difficult because in 1984 Ian and Jacky had reluctantly moved from Milburn to Sunderland. The 60-mile commute across the Pennines, via Hartside if the weather allowed, was wonderfully scenic, but after a hard day it could be testing. Ian nearly fell asleep at the wheel a couple of times. Jacky was also looking for a job.

The house Ian took on in Park Place East was, as described by Chris Mullin in his foreword, a huge, handsome terraced property built around 1850 using timbers from Sunderland shipyards. The house demanded just about everything doing to it, including a new roof which Ian proceeded to construct using the original slates. But he needed work. Luckily for him, Howard Perks had moved from Newcastle to BBC South West in Plymouth as a series producer. He recalls how he came to think about Ian, and what the results were:

"Dedicated environmental programming was almost unheard of in the late 1980s, and *Natural Concern*, the series I devised with my small team, was amongst the first of its kind. For me there was only one man to front the programmes and that was Ian. He was by far the best qualified reporter, with his unrivalled knowledge of environmental issues.

"Perhaps the most notable thing about *Natural Concern* was that the programmes were networked as a series and run mid-evening on BBC 2. I can think of no other regional series which achieved this, with the notable exception of the first couple of Keith Floyd series, which BBC South West also produced.

"*Natural Concern* covered a wide range of subjects, all fronted by Ian: +*Tarka's Troubled Water*, directed by John Hayes Fisher, was a journey down the River Torridge to observe the numerous ways it was being polluted. We know, because they told us, that this programme led directly to South West Water building more water treatment plants along the river and a change in their policies.
+*The Acid Test*, also directed by John Hayes Fisher, was the first feature report on severe water pollution at Camelford, North Cornwall, when aluminium sulphate was accidentally poured into drinking water. This is a story which still trickles on with claim and counterclaim on the legacies.

Ian's career: tv

+ *The Running of the Deer*, directed by Gary Johnston, two programmes reporting on the arguments for and against deer hunting on Exmoor. When networked we got terrific reviews for shining light rather than heat onto such an emotive issue.
+ *Katy's Birthday*, which I directed, had a big impact when networked. I had heard of a private homeopathic GP in Penzance who was driving around Cornwall with a big fibreglass tub strapped to the roof of his car. This was being used by a growing number of local women who wanted a water birth, something at that time almost unheard of in most of the country. Ian and I had to rush from Plymouth to Penzance late one evening when Katy's mum called to say she had gone into labour. After the programme there were letters published in the *Radio Times* thanking us for showing such a wonderful family event. Now there's a birthing tub in every delivery ward and Ian and I can take a tiny splash of credit for that.
+ *Death of a Farm*, directed by Janet Fraser-Cook, was a remarkable film about a Bodmin farm which had been in the same family for generations. No longer economic, it was being sold and broken up to become holiday units. The story was a vehicle for Ian to explore our relationships with the land and food production.
+ *Unnecessary Suffering?* directed by Gary Johnston, examined the way animals are treated and used as sources of food, as raw materials and as subjects for medical/scientific experimentation. It also looked at the large and growing lobby against the exploitation of animals."

   With the series completed, Ian moved to Pebble Mill, Birmingham, where he was senior reporter at *Countryfile*, the weekly magazine programme. This successful stint led to him being made, in 1989, BBC TV News environment correspondent, based at White City, London, a job he "shared" with Alex Kirby. Alex has strong memories of that partnership:
   "There always seemed to me to be something terrier-like about Ian, and I mean that as a compliment: after all, journalists are supposed to be persistent, and whatever else he may have been he was certainly that.
   "For a few years we shadowed or perhaps mirrored each other. I was the environment correspondent for BBC Radio News while he did the same job for TV News, until the time came for us to swap roles under the corporation's bi-media policy. I enjoyed tv, though I'm not certain that Ian was very happy in radio.
   "Ian was a far more experienced journalist than I was, especially in tv as

his films show so clearly, and he understood vastly more about the environment as well, but I never knew him to try to take advantage of his superiority in either sense. Quite the opposite: he was generous in sharing knowledge, contacts, expertise, and refreshments.

"Drink was part of Ian, and it could make life difficult for him, but it certainly didn't define him. It is far more Ian-as-terrier than Ian-as-imbiber that I remember.

"One demonstration of the way he would sink his teeth into a story and cling on until he'd wrestled it to a standstill was the 45-minute film on Sellafield which he made for *Panorama*. I remember him telling me that British Nuclear Fuels had been so enraged by his film that they had banned him from Sellafield for the rest of his life, an edict which didn't faze him at all."

The *Panorama* film was "A Very British Folly" about BNFL's insistence on going ahead with THORP. Broadcast on November 15 1993, it got the story right (as upheld by the Press Complaints Commission) and made the important point that commissioning THORP would trade limited profits for unlimited liabilities (as the paragraphs on pages 17-18 show). It should have been the high point of his career. Yet Ian, painstakingly polite to interviewees, had a little the look of Alec Guinness as Professor Marcus in "The Ladykillers". A troubling upper lip. Something was amiss.

23

Ian's career: tv & humanism

Like many journalists of his generation, Ian had always enjoyed a drink. For newspaper people it was the office pub round the corner; BBC staff had their own in-house clubs. Going for a drink was not just about drink, as Gerry Dempsey, former showbiz correspondent of the *Daily Express* in Manchester, commented: "My wife asked me why I had to be in pubs all the time. I said it's where you meet people and dream of ideas and intros." However, as Ian recounted in later life, "Drink mattered far more than it should. It was the drink talking, and telling John Birt exactly what I thought of him was not clever." Ian had written to the director-general in the wake of his *Panorama* film verdict demanding to know why environental stories, including ones by other journalists, were not being given air time.

"Four to five months later Chris Cramer, the BBC's head of input, called me in and thrust my letter back at me saying 'even I don't write to the DG like this - and you're on the pop again.'" Ian was grateful for the moral support of Polly Toynbee, who as social affairs editor was technically his head of department, but her memories of the event match Ian's – there was not much to be done for him. He had committed BBC suicide. His contract was not renewed.

Master of ceremonies

Back in Sunderland, doing jobs around the house, he attempted to kick the habit. It took several years, involvement with various organisations, and very firm action by Jacky before he fully regained control of himself. Luckily, he had been sober for 18 months when Jacky was discovered to have inoperable kidney cancer. Ian, together with their daughter Emmie, nursed her through her final months.

Jacky and Ian were atheists. Their 1961 marriage was a civil one at Hampstead Register Office; they lived by their own codes of respect, which included looking after Ian's mother Doris when his father Eric died in his late fifties following a stroke. Doris was not much good without Eric; Ian drove to Manchester, scooped her up and installed her in a spare room at their rented flat over the TSB opposite Crouch End clock tower in North London.

When they moved north to Milburn, Doris came too. An independent spirit, she found a job as warden of an old people's home in Carlisle, but her final years were in her own basement flat at their Sunderland house.

Jacky had requested a Humanist funeral. Ian, always the perfectionist, had been strongly involved in arrangements, though he'd had problems finding someone in the North East to take it on. Several months later, Ian was asked if he was interested in training to become a Humanist celebrant. He was. So began the third phase of his professional life.

Humanist funeral ceremonies are about the deceased, and his or her relatives and friends. Celebrants play the role of master of ceremonies. They don't normally give funeral orations. There isn't a strict Humanist line, as such. Certain poems and prose texts reinforcing universal truths are usually read. Family and friends contribute. There is music. There are moments for reflection and of course the time for committal. That's it.

The rest is not silence. It is a sensitive reconstruction – a celebration if you like - of the deceased's curriculum vitae in the context of the one sure thing about death, that it brings life to a halt. Ian became a leading practitioner of his craft.

No doubt Ian first involved himself as part of his own mourning process for Jacky. He also needed an income. After decades of making good money in newspapers and television, Ian's earning power had dropped significantly in the 1990s. While she was well enough to work, Jacky had an excellent job in the constituency office of Chris Mullin. But Park Place East was sold to pay debts and the two moved to a smaller house in another part of Sunderland.

Humanist celebrants are employed on individual commissions by funeral directors, who pay the going rate for ministers or priests. What is essentially pocket money to those with a church living may be vital to self-employed celebrants. They can hardly argue a better rate for the job because of personal circumstances. At the same time, Humanists often offer more because of the sheer effort needed to piece together someone's life when the life is the main staple of the ceremony.

During his first two and a half years as a celebrant Ian officiated at some 450 ceremonies, three or four a week, an extraordinary work rate. In his very first ceremony, back in October 1999, it is not difficult to see him thinking through his own grief:

"Death is a very personal matter for those who experience the death of someone close to them. But we are all concerned, directly or indirectly, with the death of any individual, for we are all members of one human community, and not one of us is independent and separate. Though some of the links are strong and some are tenuous, each of us is joined to all the others by links of kinship, love, friendship, by living in the same

Ian's career: humanism

neighbourhood or town or country or simply by our own common humanity."

Ian the astute social historian is also in evidence. Introducing the life of a Northumbrian working-class woman a month or two later he said:

"She was born 76 years ago. In many ways, it was a good time to be born a woman. Emancipation was becoming an approaching reality: in 1923, women sat on a divorce jury for the first time; ladies were admitted to track events at the Olympic Games; Marie Stopes opened the first women's clinic in London.

"But Britain was still coping with the heavy toll taken of its menfolk by the First World War: much of the burden of social reconstruction was borne by the country's women. And by the 1940s, when she was in her early adulthood, she was facing the same hardships as the generation of wives and mothers before her: the privations and anxiety of another world war, the austerity, the rationing, and the shortages."

Ian's original beat was the North East. His mentor was Ray Wood, the British Humanist Association's coordinator in Tyne & Wear. As Ian got more experienced in the role he increasingly differed with his colleague about approaches to funerals. This developed into a head-to-head, with the BHA in London acting as a sort of referee. The outcome was that Mr Wood left the BHA umbrella, though continuing to conduct non-religious ceremonies in the region. Ian's terrier-like nature, and sense of natural justice, had shown itself again.

He began taking more and more ceremonies in Cumbria. His daughter Emmie Short lived (and lives) in Cockermouth. For a time Ian owned a flat nearby, then he rented places into the Lake District National Park, before moving to Hexham after marrying Wendy Love in December 2007. The Cumbrian connection remained, with most of his recent work coming from funeral directors in the Carlisle/Penrith/Cockermouth areas.

Ian kept a digital file copy of each of the thousand or so ceremonies he took between 1999-2012. He rightly believed that his own up-and-down life, his experience as a marine engineer, a print and tv journalist, a music specialist, an environmental campaigner, a craftsman, a person who had faced down his own physical and emotional demons, all contributed to his ability to understand and present a life.

Talking about the Humanist approach in his slot on the BHA website, Ian wrote: "It's now no longer regarded as an irreverent or eccentric choice as the countless letters, emails and other expressions of appreciation I and other Humanist celebrants have received seem to

show. It's a choice that more and more families will be making when the time comes for them to find the right way to say farewell to the one they have lost."

Ian was himself one of the principal reasons for such growth in the North East and Cumbria. Unlike his careers with the *Guardian*, the BBC and ITV, there was to be no prompt departure, no second thoughts, no about-face. He died caring.

Ceremonies: eight lives in a thousand

A few weeks before he died in January 2013 Ian and I discussed this book project. In fact, I'd long been pressing him to write about his experiences as a Humanist celebrant, but he was always too busy preparing the next ceremony. Perhaps there was also the feeling that any semi-fictional abstraction of real life stories would be very difficult to carry off. After all, families put great trust in his tact and judgement. How would they react to recognising some element of their husband or mother reconstructed elsewhere?

With time getting shorter, Ian homed in on the scripts themselves. He picked out ceremonies from over the years and gave them to me in a digital folder simply called "Funerals for Bob".

These are the basis of the lives which follow. Obtaining permission to use them was of course the first imperative. Funeral directors, not all of whom had heard about Ian's death, provided the essential link with families (and often added kind words about Ian himself).

The eight lives have been extracted from complete ceremonies, which would usually begin with music chosen by the families. Ian's introduction would include words about humanism, and perhaps a reading from Herbert Read or Bertrand Russell. The narrative would be interspersed by music and might often include live tributes. There would be committal words and music.

It's important to point out that the people whose lives are being celebrated may not themselves have been Humanists. The common denominator is that they, or their families, have shown a preference for a non-religious funeral.

They belong to the majority who haven't during their adult lifetime participated in organised religion. For some this is a conscious choice, for others it just reflects changing patterns in society. As Ian shows in his ceremonies, their lives can be everyday. He celebrates the ordinariness of people, the fact that doing simple things well in the context of family and friends is the bedrock of society.

There were exceptions. Ian recalled one North East ceremony attended by the funeral director – and him. Another had the chief mourner handcuffed to a prison officer. Yet another, for the father of a local businessman, led to phone negotiations with the son I happened to overhear. "Yes", Ian was saying patiently, "I realise you're an important and interesting person, but the funeral is meant to be about your father, not about you."

The lives excerpted here present portraits which, Ian acknowledges, are not complete and which tend to record the points relatives most wish to be remembered, or which they are able to recall in their grief. As he put it at the end of the ceremony for Mollie Pearson Abbott (and the sentiments recur in other ceremonies):

"There are so many events and personalities that will have been left out of our narrative, quirks and characteristics that were quintessentially Mollie. But recollections and images of her will reappear, sharpen, and expand whenever you meet in the future."

During the ceremonies themselves there was, of course, a large element of participation by families and friends. Many verbal tributes have been lost. In editing the texts I have tried to keep the narrative going, and in a few instances asked closest relatives to add a few words.

Ian, I know, found a lot in the life of Charles Bray which paralleled his own. Both had come from working-class Manchester backgrounds. Charlie, as Ian calls him during the ceremony, was 18 years his senior - an important two-thirds generation of difference. But both young men left school at an early age, both loved cycling and caving, both found their way towards the top of specialist professions through brains and initiative. Both spanned the divide between science, technology and the arts, although their careers followed very different paths. Both had strong connections with Sunderland.

Ian acknowledged early in the ceremony the detailed memoir Charlie had written of his eventful life. Obviously Ian called on this memoir, which doesn't mean his achievement at summarising Charlie's life is any less remarkable. Journalists use the best available source material; the art lies in drawing the strands together, making sense and holding interest while not bending the story.

Three lives – Julie Broadhurst, Karen Foulds and Debbie Godsey – are women who died young; young, that is, by the tally of Charles Bray. Ian shows, through painstaking and sensitive character recreation, how each individual personality impacted on the lives of their family and friends – and how they are remembered by those closest to them. In these instances, like Jacky, Ian's first wife, their lives were tragically foreshortened by illness.

Two other lives, those of Leslie Halliman and Peter Johnston, who also died young by today's standards, are men who quietly made positive differences to those around them. Ian builds up, brick by brick, a faithful replica of their personalities, their careers, their families, their friends and the communities in which they lived. With Mollie Pearson Abbott and Hetty Baron-Thieme, women who lived long and fulfilling lives, he lets their record speak for themselves, aided and abetted by friends and relatives. Sometimes you can hear the spontaneity of the spoken word rather than the written judgement. So be it. Ian creates word and mind pictures of his subjects, imagining himself into their very beings. The celebrations live on beyond the funeral ceremonies. For those of us who weren't there, they are a privileged insight into 'other lives'.

Ian brought a newspaperman's interviewing skills and a television presenter's unflappability to the funeral event, arranging music and quotations, checking facts with relatives, phoning those who couldn't be there, writing scripts to exact length, so that ceremonies – usually under time pressure at the crematorium – took place with minimum stress and maximum dignity. And, it has to be said, with a warmth of spirit not always apparent amongst celebrants of whatever stripe.

Four of the following life stories were conducted after October 2011, when Ian learned that he had inoperable lung cancer. He'd been a heavy cigarette smoker until giving up on his 60th birthday in September 2000 – but, as he admitted, that wasn't soon enough. During the chemotherapy and follow-up treatment, which he undertook with typical thoroughness, he did his best to continue working.

What irritated him most was the fact that his dentist seemed unable to prescribe satisfactory false teeth to allow him to look and sound the part for ceremonies. In the final months he was increasingly dependent on Wendy to drive him. But most people didn't guess he was dying.

Ian never lost his sense of humour. He liked to recall how he was once paid in used fivers by a funeral director within sight of grieving relatives, but how he took the cash all the same. Sometimes, after an interview session, the nearest and dearest would say to him:

"We like the Humanist way of doing things but can't we just have a little prayer as well?"

"No."

There are limits to a Humanist's tolerance.   **Robert Waterhouse**

Mollie Pearson Abbott   1928-2007

Mollie was born in 1928 at Peebles but taken to live in Edinburgh when she was still a toddler. Precise details of her early childhood are hazy: what we do know is that she was a bubbly, happy little girl who loved games, running, swimming, and – no surprise – who did well at school. Those who think of the Scottish education system as one of rounded superiority to its English counterpart would see Mollie and her progress through that system as an exemplar.

In any event, she went to the Mary Erskine School in Edinburgh, where she imbibed a respect for classical learning as well as an intolerance for slovenly speech and writing, and where she became heavily involved in the games and gymnastics that were to shape the rest of her life. Her PE teacher at the school was Helen Rintoul, who regarded Mollie as her star pupil and who later would ask her to become godmother to her three children – one of whom, the actor David Rintoul, we will hear from later.

Mollie's character as a student was not unlike that for which she was known when she herself was a lecturer and an administrator. There's a Latin phrase that might have been coined for her: *Ne tentes aut perfice* – "if it's worth doing, it's worth doing well". As a pupil at Dunfermline College, where she enrolled just as the war ended, she was self-possessed, hardworking, cheerful – and a natural achiever. She qualified and left to teach in various Edinburgh schools before becoming a lecturer, at the age of only 24, at Moray House College of Education.

Her progress from that point onwards was outstanding, especially in a world, even that of education, which was run and ruled by men. Mollie, never aggressively feminist or zealously reformist, nonetheless overturned that and many other bastions of the old order. And for all that she accomplished then and later, she never became pompous or self-important. But the real importance of what Mollie did over the years of her career can't be exaggerated. She helped to bring about a transformation in the practice and principles of physical education.

Her manner, assertive, confident, reasonable and logical, underpinned with a sense of humour that was just as devastating as any excoriation, was hugely productive and creative. Everything Mollie did was focused on the students and what their educational attainments would do for the wider community. She applied an inclusivity to physical education that might seem obvious now but which was bravely novel when she expounded it. Health and fitness, enjoyment of sport, provision for disability – she integrated them.

Not only was Mollie at the centre of the new thinking which saw a wider relevance to physical education, but she was developing her strengths as a campaigner for schools and colleges under threat – whatever they taught. After her time at Moray College, Mollie worked at Ripon, then as principal lecturer at Aberdeen College of Further Education, before being appointed to Her Majesty's Inspectorate of Schools in 1964. At the age of only 36, Mollie took on a responsibility she was to discharge with vigour and enterprise.

> 'Not only was Mollie at the centre of the new thinking which saw a wider relevance to physical education, but she was developing her strengths as a campaigner for schools and colleges under threat'

But, as her partner Jean and everyone else who has known Mollie would be quick to point out, there was, amongst all this serious stuff, no shortage of fun, often directed at herself. She travelled a lot, of course, and drove countless miles, especially in those early days of moving between Scotland and Yorkshire or London.

On one occasion, long before the M6 was built, she was struggling through a winter white-out on Shap – notorious for immobilising everything when the blizzards struck. Spotting a vehicle by the side of the road, Mollie pulled over and shouted at a figure she could dimly see through the flakes: "Can I help you?" A voice replied "You help *me*? This is a snow plough!"

In 1970, after her appointment as an inspector came to an end, Mollie returned as principal to the college where she had begun her career –

Dunfermline, known to its alumni and friends as Dunf. It was now in purpose-built premises. Just after Mollie arrived a new extension was due to be opened by the Queen Mother, who was escorted by the outgoing principal, Miss Blunden. Mollie was to accompany the then Secretary of State for Scotland, Willie Ross.

As they made their decorous progress around the school, Mollie said: "Now, this is the new swimming pool," and ceremoniously flung open a door – to reveal a toilet. The Secretary of State replied: "Mmm. It's a little smaller than I'd have expected."

Needless to say, Mollie was a formidable committee woman and the natural choice as chair on some of the most powerful education bodies, to which she brought her wit and vision. We haven't by any means exhausted what there is to say about the rich professional contribution Mollie made, but humour, fun, and sociability were central to her life – so how appropriate at this point in our celebration of her life to be able call on her godson, David Rintoul, currently starring in the West End production of Dirty Dancing:

"Mollie was godmother to my sister Do, my brother Dougie and me. She took being our godmother seriously – lightly but seriously – and she was very much part of our family and part of our lives as we grew up," David said.

"Her role came about thus: our mother Helen was a student at Dunfermline College at the outbreak of the Second World War when the college was moved up to Aberdeen, where our parents met. Shortly after mum qualified, she found herself as a very young head of PE at the Mary Erskine School in Edinburgh where Mollie was a star pupil. There was an age difference of only around six years; they became friends, Mollie herself went to Dunf, and when our father came back from the war and our parents married, Mollie was a bridesmaid and subsequently our godmother.

"We saw a lot of Mollie during our childhoods. We often stayed in Edinburgh with Mollie and the redoubtable Mrs Abbott – mother to Mollie and to Barry – in Barnton Terrace. We always looked forward to seeing Mollie because she was fun to be with. She had a certain raciness; she had glamour.

"She also had a natural empathy with young people of all ages. My sister Do and Mollie had a ritual together. Shortly after she arrived for a visit Mollie was required to act out Cinderella in its entirety, with Mollie playing – naturally – the Fairy Godmother and the infant Do playing every other part.

"Much later, when I was a student at Edinburgh, I remember late night

Mollie Pearson Abbott

sessions in the front room at Barnton Terrace sitting on the carpet – she generally preferred the carpet to furniture – smoking, drinking whisky, talking about everything under the sun and arguing. Mollie liked an argument. She was a bonnie fechter.

"Looking at Mollie's life from a *Who's Who* perspective – HM Inspector of Schools, Principal of Dunfermline College, member of the Scottish Arts Council, Commander of the Order of the British Empire – you would probably conclude 'Redoubtable Scottish Woman. Pillar of the Establishment'. Redoubtable Scottish Woman, certainly. Pillar of the Establishment? Too much her own woman for that, I think.

"When Jean retired she and Mollie moved to Janefield, their house in Kirkudbright with its beautiful but demanding garden. They had, I think, a happy time there together – not only there but on visits to the Italian lakes and skiing – but it wasn't an idle time. They delivered meals on wheels, ran the mobile library, gave a lot of their time and energy to the local community ... If you divide humanity into the givers and the takers, Mollie was high of the list of the givers.

"I saw Mollie last week, shortly before she died. It was a bright, clear day and we sat in the sitting room looking out on the fine view over Morecambe Bay. She wasn't in good physical shape but her spirit was as strong as ever – in charge of her own life, interested in other people, dry, witty, amusing, amused.

"To have lived a good life to a good age, to die leaving love and respect in the hearts of so many people, is not, in any way, a tragedy. And yet. The sadness and loss that we all feel give us some understanding of what you, Jean, her dear companion and partner, must be going through. I don't know if it's any comfort to know that your grief is shared, Jean. I hope it is."

There have been – of course, scores of letters, e-mails, phone calls and visits from friends and former colleagues, students, and members of Jean's family, all with messages of support for her and warm recollections of Mollie. The Edinburgh lawyer on the governing body of Dunf writes of her being an "outstanding" member of her profession. A London friend recalls her "wit, her style, and her hospitality." And Duncan, a close friend of Mollie's brother, talks of the "aura of cheerfulness" surrounding her.

Mollie's major contribution to education – in Scotland and on wider academic horizons beyond the Border – was sealed during the period of her being principal at Dunf, from 1970 to 1983. She widened the range of competent staff and enlarged the curriculum. From being a college that trained women teachers of physical education, it came to offer courses in leisure studies, in sports coaching, in outdoor pursuits, fitness training, and in work with disabled people. Dunf also grew into being an important centre for physical fitness and recreational activities.

These years also saw Mollie as a tireless crusader for all that was worthwhile in education, and a defender of any part of it that was under political or economic threat. She became a well-known lobbyist down at Westminster, promoting and protecting educational standards and facilities, arm-twisting MPs and civil servants.

At one point, Mollie was simultaneously fighting against the merger of the college and opposing the extension of Edinburgh Airport. She spent a great deal of time in London during these years. Back in Edinburgh, and on more than one occasion, Mollie would be spearheading protest marches on St Andrew's House, flags and music and all. Staff and students alike rallied to her calls.

'She would hold meetings each term at which she would lay down the law, leaving no one unscathed. Then she would say something that had everyone rolling around'

Wendy Binnie, who succeeded Mollie in the inspectorate, says "she was professionally fearless. If there was an injustice, she'd fight to right it. And with that, went her talent for leadership." That history of hers, and comments like Wendy's, help to explain why Mollie's charismatic and distinguished career led, at her retirement, to being made a CBE – an award which, typically, she regarded as a badge of honour for her students as much as for herself.

Far more important in her own life was the fact that this period at Dunf in the 1970s saw her meet Jean Carroll and form with her the loving partnership that was to last her lifetime. Jean, appointed by Mollie as head of department in 1973, brought to Dunf, after a varied career in teaching in schools and colleges and further training and study, her specialist knowledge in sociology and in the social aspects of movement. The professional respect and affection they had for one another would grow as they both developed in their respective roles. Jean, who was to become vice principal, recalls both the serious and the decidedly unserious sides to Mollie at work.

Mollie Pearson Abbott

She would hold meetings each term at which she would lay down the law unambiguously, leaving no one unscathed. Then she would say something that had everyone rolling around in mirth. She developed her views and her plans for honours degree courses in PE, the diversification into sports coaching, creative dance and other curricular innovations. But at the end of the college day, it was her wee dram that mattered more than her syllabus.

Mollie was an inspiration to all who worked with her or studied under her: of that there's not a shadow of a doubt, and it's that quality that is crystallised for us now by Ellen Boyle.

Ellen says:

"I felt it was perhaps appropriate to call this reflection 'From Ms Abbott to Mollie'. I am in the privileged position of talking about Ms Abbott (the Principal of Dunfermline College of PE) and Mollie my friend – which spans a period of 35 years.

"I had hoped to be joined by Professor Nanette Mutrie of the University of Strathclyde who, like me, was a student at Dunfermline College of PE. Unfortunately she couldn't make it but sent some comments which are encompassed in what I have to say.

"For those of you who don't know, being a "Dunfer" is, was, pretty special, especially in the era when it was run by Mollie Abbott. I'd say that more PE teachers in Scotland – if you scratch the surface – are likely to have memories of Mollie or heard about her.

"Why – you might ask – was it so special? It was to do with the culture, the ethos, the values that Mollie brought to Dunf.

"The very fact that I am here giving this address, with my Glasgow, working-class, Catholic, East End, large comprehensive school background is in itself a sort of testimony to the kind of changes that Mollie brought to the world of physical education. In 1970 she took over the principalship of Dunf and immediately began opening up the student and educational experience. We set off with her (my year intake of the young women Mollie had selected and interviewed) and we discovered a formidable and visionary leader who cared about physical education and about our lives.

"She created a learning environment that was both nurturing and inspirational. She was a role model for us young women – enabling us to believe in ourselves, and to go out confidently and do what we wanted.

"Many went on to do great work; not only in the PE field but in different professions and this stemmed from the roots, from the rich, compassionate education we received – and that in itself developed a huge affection for Dunf and for Mollie. But also it was exciting and fun.

"Within that time Mollie had developed the first B Ed course which also brought other academic professionals onto the staff at Dunf – and indeed my friendship with Jean was cemented through the creation of the new sociology dept. Those were heady times. I remember Mollie's pleasure in the "consultation process with students" about who we should invite to confer this momentous degree – and the delight in making it happen – that the Duke of Edinburgh himself led the ceremony.

"Mollie was at ease in anyone's company – be it the Duke himself (the Queen later), the students, the kitchen staff, the janitor. It didn't matter. She was just Mollie: warm, upbeat, direct. She knew who she was and this was inculcated in her students. For me, that's the greatest gift you can offer anyone. But even when she was principal, with all the 'seriousness' that entailed, she'd have lots of fun. Not everyone will know of the brilliant  performance given by her, Dr MacLean and Jean as the reconstructed Gary Glitter Band.

"I maintained my connection with Mollie and Jean, and Marion Woodward and I have had 20 years of great friendship with them. They inspired us in their retirement. They constructed how they wanted to live and they enjoyed it to the full. Mollie was fun to be with and she truly embraced life right to the end. She lived it to the full and enjoyed her

Mollie Pearson Abbott

retirement in Kircudbright and Grange-over-Sands as much as her professional life.

"Because she knew who she was she was as happy in the background as she'd been at the forefront of things, delivering meals on wheels, as a shop assistant in the charity shop, or, as I dearly remember her, in her solid support of Jean and I who would usually arrive last in our 10k races.

"Mollie enjoyed people and she took pleasures from so many things; her holidays, her vegetables, her soups, her computer, her gadgets, her garden, her bell-ringing, her discussions and debates (she gave you a real run for your money in an argument, especially if she'd had a couple of whiskies). She was a very generous person who loved to welcome people to her home. She always welcomed you with open arms, a big smile, and in our particular case a lovely glass of sherry. She was happy with our life and though we are sad today that she is gone, she'd want us to remember her in the happy times that permeated her life.

"I think it was Maya Angelou who said – the really sad thing is a life not lived. And there is no way we can say that about Mollie."

When Mollie finally retired it was only from paid employment at Dunf. It wasn't from all the other interests and activities that had energised and filled her life and, increasingly, that of Jean as well. Mollie stayed in Edinburgh for three years. Concerts, plays, cinema and good food all played a part in their lives before they decided to move. Looking in the *Scotsman* for a house of their own, they spotted a property in Kirkcudbright – and thought they'd drive out and take a look.

They looked no further, for Janefield House was the perfect place to turn into their home, which it was for more than 13 very happy years. They had a swimming pool, they walked and played golf; they went abroad; Mollie learned the finer points of using computers; she also took up handbell ringing, joining a local group after hearing them play one Christmas. The group gave performances in residential homes and other venues, and Mollie managed to get the lottery fund to part with money for a second set of bells.

She made many new friends – as she always did wherever she went. And she and Jean went abroad often – langlaufing in Switzerland and Austria and, on Lake Garda, windsurfing, a sport which Mollie insisted she'd try having watched a party of women from Munich speed across the water. If German women can do it, then so can we, she declared. And so they did.

They travelled to the US a couple of times, visited Hong Kong, where Jean's niece Sara has spent a lot of time, and China. Mollie, who spoke good French, was keen to learn Spanish and was going to have taken lessons for planned trips later this year to Spain and Mallorca.

There was no stopping her – especially not the swimming, which she was doing only weeks ago in the pool they had built beneath the house at Grange. When they moved there, Mollie had taken up golf once again, becoming, no surprise, Ladies Captain of the Grange Fell Club. And it was through the club that she met Liz Casling, who now recounts her memories of Mollie.

"My husband Terry and I met M&J in the latter stage of Mollie's life in Grange-over-Sands. Discovery of shared backgrounds in physical education (Jean and I went to the same teacher training college) sparked a connection that developed into a close and much valued friendship.

"Mollie's sardonic observations of events past and present provided endless fuel for merriment. For all her wealth of experience, knowledge and remarkable life achievements Mollie lacked any sense of vanity – indeed sought every opportunity to celebrate and encourage the qualities and successes of others she respected.

"A trait I took particular delight in was her pragmatism and wonderful barbed wit – a consummate professional when it came to deflating enlarged egos and pomposity. Mollie certainly did not suffer fools gladly.

"One very memorable and now sadly poignant evening was spent last autumn going over M&J's 'Just in Case' instructions prior to a pending trip abroad. What really should have been a most serious subject (who to contact in case of joint fatality due to air crash, terrorism etc) became, as always, a light-hearted sharing of memories and anecdotes, albeit funereal ones!

"To ease the responsibility and stress for family and friends, nothing was to be left to chance – all arrangements and locations precisely listed – including pre-recorded music and appropriate readings."

Mollie was fond of Jean's nieces Sara and Helly. Helly describes Mollie as a wonderful woman who was assertive but always, friendly, kind and hospitable. Sara, whose children Charlotte, Lucy and Ben had all grown to love Mollie, reports that Lucy sent a card to Westmorland General, telling Mollie what a brave and courageous woman she was. Mollie laughed out loud at the very idea. She didn't think she was brave.

Mollie's partnership with Jean was made formal last year. At first they didn't think it was necessary to do that. After all, no one – most importantly the two of them – needed any official seal to be set on their love for one another. But someone asked what would happen if one of you had to go into hospital or something, and they might not let the other one in? So they had an affirmation at Kendal Register Office, and afterwards they took their witnesses, Sara and Helly, for a meal at L'Enclume in Cartmel. You get the impression that, like the meal in the West End after Mollie had collected her CBE from Buckingham Palace, the fun and enjoyment of the day was far more important than the ceremony.

There are so many events and personalities that will have been left out of our narrative, quirks and characteristics that were quintessentially Mollie. But recollections and images of her will reappear, sharpen, and expand whenever you meet in the future.

The funeral ceremony for Mollie Pearson Abbott CBE was held at Carlisle Crematorium on Thursday March 15 2007

Julie Broadhurst

1958-2008

Eric and Cynthia Brook, Julie's parents, lived on a boat moored on the River Soar in Leicestershire. The St George, an historic vessel restored by Eric after his service in the Navy and Fleet Air Arm, was a wonderful home for Julie, their first-born, who looked back on her childhood with great affection and happiness. It was an environment in which her giving nature, her artistic and practical talents and her spirit of enterprise all flourished.

Thus she drew and painted, sailed and narrow-boated on the rivers and canals of the East Midlands, Fenland, the Bristol Channel, and abroad in Belgium, learned to recognise the wild and plant life of the places they visited, and completed her schooling with an expeditionary project in a dinghy on the disused Grantham canal.

Even as a youngster, Julie had the educator's instinct. Her father recalls that she'd line up young friends as pupils, with herself in front as the teacher. Apparently, she would sternly discipline her little brother Roger if he dared to talk or failed to pay attention in her class – an image that would surely strike a chord, decades later, with some of her students at Ullswater Community College.

The caring, conscientious side of Julie was also evident in those early years: she liked to help with ironing and cooking, she played a part in planning family trips. And she enjoyed life – decorating the boat for Christmas, dancing, listening to birdsong, relishing the sights and sounds of rivers and harbours, and discovering the delights of textiles and fabrics, their colours, patterns and textures, the love of which was to define so much of her future.

In 1977 Julie completed a foundation year at Loughborough School of Art, where she met Stuart Broadhurst – the man she was to marry. She also met and made lasting friendships like the one with Travers Bell, who recalls that she was self-possessed, diligent, a gifted draftswoman, patient and cheerful. She was, he says, a special person who seemed to have a good

Julie Broadhurst

idea of what she wanted to do – and it included helping others to do well.

She went to Birmingham University, studying fine art and textile design and leaving with a first class honours degree. Even before she graduated, she was headhunted for a lecturing post at North Staffs Polytechnic in Stoke on Trent – a job she took after a period living in mid-Kent with Stuart. Two children, Ferg and Eve, had been born in the 1980s before the family moved north and settled in Temple Sowerby, where they began a barn conversion.

That – like every enterprise on which Julie embarked – brought out all that was clever and imaginative in her. She could work as happily and constructively with a mix of mortar as with a bolt of cloth. She became, for a while, a multitalented mainstay in the building business she and Stuart ran.

'Julie could work as happily and as constructively with a mix of mortar as with a bolt of cloth'

She loved materials, found new uses for discarded items, made things that were beautiful and useful, combined function and form in the way that defines good design. Her craft skills were outstanding and so was her drawing. But most important, says her great and close friend Sarah Braithwaite, was that she never sought praise or applause for her work. In fact she thought her efforts were nothing special.

Others disagree. Sarah, herself an accomplished artist, thought Julie's artistic work extraordinary, and so within a short time of her settling in the Eden Valley did the staff and students at Ullswater Community College, where Julie began working as a technician and eventually became an extraordinarily valued teacher. The head of the art department at UCC, Owen Smith, says that pupils would do anything for her – they tried hard to repay what she did for them.

She would work long hours in the evenings and at weekends, preparing and inventing, improvising and developing ideas and practical components for the students' projects. Owen writes:

"Julie was the most wonderful person to work with; highly enthusiastic, compassionate, inspirational, supportive – the list is endless. My overriding memory is of laughter and joy. She approached her teaching very much from a maternal direction and just couldn't help herself looking after everyone she came into contact with. She always thought of others first.

There are countless students who have benefited from her caring attitude and many who would have fallen by the wayside if it hadn't been for her unswerving support. She was an exceptional practitioner; highly skilled, she also had the ability to pass on her expertise to aspiring artists. The quality of work she got from students was in many cases outstanding. She taught them to be ambitious and creative. Students had a strong bond and warmth towards her . . . she was also a great friend who saw me through difficult times and supported many other members of staff."

What a testament that is. And just as powerful is this, written by Julie's great friend and colleague Nikki, who so very much wanted to be here today but is visiting her daughter in Japan. This is her tribute to Julie:

"Julie, I feel that we have always been friends but I knew you only for the last 12 years. We were colleagues, but became friends when you began helping with the school productions at UCC. You gave your time, as with everything else, so generously. Your imagination and genuine love for all the arts and for the young people involved revealed themselves in the sureness of your touch – whether you painted an old chair powder blue and then 'distressed' it, placed a potted plant in exactly the same position on stage night after night or mended a torn costume, still being worn, in two minutes between scenes. You loved going to the theatre and, often accompanying me and students, revelled in the event.

"Some thought you were a 'soft touch', indeed you were one of the kindest and most empathetic people I have met, but you had another side: I have been present when you reprimanded students – your righteous anger and the power of its expression left them and me in no doubt at all! You were an awesome teacher – that's not the skewed vision of a friend but the conclusion of your tutors who, so recently, awarded you full teacher status after you completed your training 'on the job'. You were thorough, passionate and you had integrity, as well as an imaginative strength which was impossible to ignore.

"I have never heard anyone say a negative word about you, Julie. You made friends of everyone, even those who didn't quite understand you or who thought you a little 'alternative'. As one student put it to you (and you delighted in quoting this): a bit 'knit your own sausages'. Actually, if it could be done, you'd have done it. You did once make some beautiful Christmas cards out of baked bean tins. I fondly remember how you once showed me how to make felt and together we made Christmas presents. The brooches I made and gave away made me so proud and you gave of your time and expertise so gladly to the rest of us.

Julie Broadhurst

"Julie, you loved all aspects of life: shopping for clothes and getting your hair coloured; you loved animals – Mike bought you three hens you delighted in and you had two greedy ginger cats, Spike and Alfie. You often came to us for a 'dose of dog' as you described it. You were the only person to tolerate my slobbery dog's ministrations.

"You loved the countryside, and especially the seaside – a walk beside the sea was always great therapy for you. A few years ago, when living in Wordsworth Street and without a garden you took on the allotment. It had a blue and yellow shed where we kept a kettle and mugs, chairs and more flowers than veg. It was a place for contemplation and socialising. In true Jules fashion, you weren't there for what you could get out of it. You were there!

"Nothing was done by halves. When someone needed your help, they got it. You drove friends great distances if they need a lift and counselled at great length those in distress. You committed yourself to others with love and enormous kindness.

"Jules, of all the places you liked to be home was the best. Wherever you lived became quickly suffused with your magic – a touch comprising a brilliant imagination, visual awareness, an appetite for beauty and care for the comfort of anyone who might be in your home no matter for how short a time.

"You loved parties, and the parties that you and Mike gave became legendary – fairy lights (literally hundreds of them), barbecues, music and a mix of people of all ages, in fancy dress or not.

"You loved preparing food for others and sharing it. A great pride for you was the table that Mike made. You quickly dressed it beautifully and were never so happy as when it was surrounded by family and friends eating the food you had prepared.

"For one who loved life so much and appreciated the gifts of every single day right up to the last day granted to you, it seems very cruel that you saw so few. But Julie, what your life lacked in length, was surely made up for in depth.

"Thank you, Julie, for your great gifts and for all the love you gave to so many – Nikki."

What a wonderful account of a friendship.

Before becoming a tutor in textiles at UCC, Julie had worked briefly at Lilliput Lane in Penrith. Very briefly, for as someone noted, prolonged exposure to the crafts on show there might have driven her to distraction or even destruction, though she wasn't by nature an arts fascist. In fact,

Julie, for all that she had some strong views, was quintessentially tolerant: it was part of a generosity of spirit which marked her out in just about everything she did.

As most of you know, Julie and Stuart were eventually to go their own separate ways, but not without leaving many good and happy memories and, of course, the legacy of two loved and talented children. Julie was very proud that Eve followed her into the world of art and textiles.

After meeting Mike, there was to be a new family. They soon became, almost seamlessly, another vital part of her life. They also recognised that what she loved most of all was seeing others enjoying themselves. How else to account for the joy she derived from having twelve to dinner as often as she could, laying on food and drink and music, radiating her own pleasure to produce delight and happiness in everyone around her.

And that thought is that leads naturally to the recounting of the new chapter in Julie's life – the period of loving partnership she shared with Mike and his three grown-up children, Tess, Nick and Tom.

'For all that she had strong views, Julie was quintessentially tolerant: it was part of a generosity of spirit'

Tess says this: "I was lucky enough to know Jules as a teacher, a mother and a friend. She was the warmest, most caring person, who had an amazing ability to put anyone at ease, and make a rather bad situation good. I travelled to Australia and became ill while out there. Jules wrote me a letter when this happened. She finished it with 'Always look to the future, Tess. Life is great really, these little blips make us forget.' This was so special to me, and made me look at life differently.

"Talking about her stubborness and how proud she was of the life she created when our families moved in together, dad had this old brick with Ashwin carved into it which he placed at the back door; on seeing this, Jules quickly got a brick she found in the back yard, grabbed a black marker pen and scribbled BROADHURST on it, which she placed above our brick. It was extremely funny. Anyway that was the beginning of the Broadwins, or the Ashhursts.

"Although this is a horrible time, in some ways we are the luckiest families in the world, because we were brought together. Towards the end of Jules's illness what she liked most of all, she told me, was listening to us younger

Julie Broadhurst

generation all around her just living, and enjoying life. Even if she was sleeping she wanted to have us around her.

"I know Humanists don't believe in life after death, or heaven, but a couple of weeks ago on a particularly bad day I sat by the bed with her, and she told me she wasn't scared about death, because she was going see Carly, my best friend at school who we lost in the terrible road accident three years ago - and that made me feel comforted.

"Jules changed all of our lives, and watching dad care for Jules over the time made me realise just how deeply in love they were, they had so many plans. She changed dad in ways that only he will know. But I see a difference, he is a calmer person, he was able to stop and enjoy life, something he never could really do before Jules."

Mike's mother Lucy and sisters Sue and Wendy send these warm thoughts:

"Jules's beauty and generosity of spirit gave us so much happiness. She knew the true value of things, and the tenderness which Mike and Jules showed towards each other was a measure of their great love for one another. It has been a privilege to have known and loved her and her family too."

Julie was a friend and confidant to anyone who needed her. Encouraging, supportive, warm, she made a difference, as this note from Nick makes clear.

"Something Jules said often when we discussed my plans or progress was 'There's no point in doing or getting involved in anything you don't enjoy.' It's said by lots of other people too, but I really listened when Jules said it, because she proved its meaning every day by enjoying everything she did with dad."

Julie never forgot the fun she had in her university years, never aged in her outlook or lost the wonderment of the new, the exciting, the shocking and original.

Julie's concern for others was boundless – and it was a characteristic that went right back to her youth and her twenties. One Christmas, not long after she was married and having joined her parents for Christmas dinner, she served up a meal of bread and cheese. The money she saved went for Famine Relief.

Julie refused to admit that she had any particularly attractive attributes. She even described herself as plain – when the only thing that was plain was that she was stunningly good-looking.

She was uncomplaining in her illness, resolved to live as fully and for as long as possible and determined, almost madly so, to lead as normal a life as she could. To their credit, and her joy, both Ferg and Eve graduated from university during this difficult time.

The day of Ferg's graduation ceremony at Liverpool University she walked, on legs that theoretically weren't strong enough to support a kitten, the long stretch between the Anglican and Catholic cathedrals. Two days later, she was in hospital, having a hip operation and being told that her leg could have shattered at any time.

Julie loved travelling, adored Harris in the Outer Hebrides and Eskdale in the South Lakes. And of course, she was practically a physical part of Bluebell the Camper van that took her and the family to so many places and in which she recorded, in her inimitable handwriting and sketches in wonderful bound diaries, everything they were doing and the places they were visiting. France, Scotland, the North Country. So many memorable trips are made even more memorable through her graphic accounts of them.

There are sure to be many other stories, other chapters, numerous episodes in Julie's life that we have overlooked today – the laughs, the magical films she loved, the paintings she did, the champagne that added to her own natural sparkle. But we have tried to bring out some of the essence of what made her what she was, the woman you cared for.

The funeral ceremony for Julie Broadhurst was held at Beacon Edge Woodland, Penrith Cemetery, on Thursday June 12 2008

Karen Foulds

1956-2011

Karen was one of two children born to Ray and Margot Foulds:
Ray was a teacher originally from Bacup in Lancashire and Margot
had come to Britain as a Jewish refugee from Germany. So
Karen's upbringing, in Pooley Bridge, was inevitably touched by
humanitarian values, a rejection of intolerance, and the natural
development of an inquiring mind that would never let presumptions go
unchallenged.

Karen's brother Peter, a year or so her older, recalls a sister who was
consumed with a love of animals. She had a dog then and had several
others later in her life – and also took naturally to horses, confidently riding
and pony-trekking around Ullswater and helping out at a riding school in
Glenridding.

From an early age, certainly by the time she was a pupil at Yanwath
Primary, she was drawn to the pen, the pencil and the brush. Her talents
for painting and sketching were pronounced, and art was one of the
subjects in which she excelled at Penrith Grammar, where she also did well
in English. She liked writing, was articulate, and was acquiring a keen sense
of what it is that differentiates the way things are from what they could
and should be. Well before she left grammar school she had a passion for
justice and for righting wrong.

She went for a time to Chester College, an early foray into the world of
teaching or at least teacher training, but Karen wasn't ready for that – or
for any formal career at that point. She was a free spirit, a child who'd
grown up in the 1960s and had the feel for nature that those years spent
among the eastern fells had imbued in her. For a time, Karen lived in Bristol
as part of a squat – which was not uncommon in the early 1970s but which
her brother Peter remembers thinking was a very hippy existence.

The fact is that Karen never would be a prisoner of convention; her
innate social conscience probably impelled her to look around at the world
and ask what convention had ever done for those who fell foul of the
system. She was developing what Marion Smith, a great friend in later life,
would describe as a ferocious determination to defend the abused, the
denied, the short-changed. Not long after leaving Bristol and returning to
Cumbria, Karen became a nurse.

That wasn't the first thing she did. For a time, she worked as a landscape
architect: the details are a little hazy, but it was work that took her to the
Cockermouth area, and shortly afterwards, around 1982, she met Clem
Shaw. Their first encounter was at a jazz club in Keswick, and it's not hard
to see what drew them so quickly and powerfully together. She was, quite

48

Karen Foulds

simply, stunningly attractive. More than that: she glowed with a passion for change and challenge in what she saw as an unfair world, radiating a determination to do something for those in need. Clem, a presenter with Border Television, was a fellow radical spirit.

So it was all but a foregone conclusion that they should become a couple within a short time of that first chance meeting. At some stage, Karen had moved into the famous purple house in the Newlands Valley – Rigg Beck – a house so eccentric and special and which eventually fell down under its own neglected bulk. In those days, it was a place for dreamers and idealists, and Karen and Clem took one of the flats in the house.

But what Karen embarked on then was no idealistic dream. It was the very practical and self-sacrificing role as a mental nurse for which she trained and worked in Dovenby Hall, which then had 400 patients. She was there for a couple of years before – and again the exact chronology is fuzzy – the couple moved to Carlisle. Clem was now working as a producer and getting serious films made; Karen was pregnant with their daughter Jenny, who would be half-sister to Clem's little girl Becky.

They settled in Chiswick Street, in a fine Victorian house that everyone loved but which was to be home for a tantalisingly short time. Karen saw an advertisement for a postgraduate course in art therapy in St Albans, applied, and was accepted. Clem, who'd been freelance for a while and was about to run his own tv production company, welcomed the chance to live within commuting distance of London. And so they moved.

Karen flourished on her course, but in other ways, she wilted. The South – even a county as attractive as Hertfordshire – wasn't for her. She missed the valleys and fells. In addition, Karen's mother Margot was ill and deteriorating.

So they came back, moved to live in Lady Rigg Farm, and Karen rose to new challenges. She was to look after her mother – and later her father – but was also freelancing as a carer and an art therapist: the two activities overlapped and were complementary. She dealt with some extraordinarily difficult and wretched cases of abuse as part of her case load.

Children sent to Cumbria from Manchester and other big cities were among the worst cases. She gave them comfort, hope, opened up possibilities and horizons that must have been the spiritual equivalent of food for the starving. She was, as so many of her friends and colleagues have said, inspirational. It's an adjective that has fallen victim to overuse, but in Karen's case, was true: she restored many children, in Clem's words, to a state approaching normality.

She could be open and generous in ways they'd never experienced. And in addition to this work for local authorities, Karen worked in NHS care homes, from Carlisle to Newcastle, combining all this with her own work as an artist. It is hard to believe how much she crammed into her life over these years, but it is believable because so many here today saw her do it. And – as her children all say – she always, always put other people first.

Tim, born in 1987, remembers a mother who was unstoppably engaged with her work, with what he and his sisters were doing, with her painting and photography, her music, her dog, with anything and everything that drew on her passions and her skills. They had moved from Lady Rigg Farm to Maughanby Farm, and it was while she was living there that Karen met Marianne Henry outside the gates at Langwathby primary school, where Jenny and Verity May were pupils.

That was the beginning of an exceptional friendship. The children were part of the amalgam, of course, but so were shared feelings for justice and commonsense, for art and beauty, for music, for thinking.

'Like many a good atheist, Karen was fond of ecclesiastical buildings and ruins, appreciating the great architecture, music and art funded by the worshipful'

Marianne and Karen both had a commitment to the Greenham Common cause: they believed passionately that it was wrong for our country to give haven to weapons of mass destruction and their commanding forces; they linked their arms in peace around that infamous camp; they campaigned among the indifferent citizens of Penrith and won the arguments if not the battle, in which – ultimately - they were the victors by default.

Marianne remembers the caravan parked in the yard at Maughanby, has images of the pond, the garden which Karen tended with characteristic proficiency, can still see her with Miss Helen and Max, and speaks of Addingham Church nearby. Like many a good atheist, Karen was fond of ecclesiastical buildings and ruins, appreciated the great architecture, music and art that have been funded over the centuries by the worshipful.

The children were happy: it was an idyllic time, even for grown-ups, says Marianne: they swapped plants, drank espresso coffee, laughed a lot. Jenny and Verity made up sketches, put on shows that were over-the-top extensions of French and Saunders; they cast poor little Tim as the offspring, carried him round the garden cooing, with Karen and Marianne

Karen Foulds

caricatured as idealistic earth mothers.

What made Karen so special, made her the person you all remember so fondly and vividly, is that she synthesised so completely and creatively all the facets of life that concerned or interested her. Her compassion, her sense of humour, her technical dexterity, her command of art, photography and sculpture, her pacifism (a pacifism not to be diluted by or confused with her assertive personality) her music, and finally her feminism – all came together in every enterprise.

So, Karen's work with the women's refuge in Carlisle was a product of all these qualities. Her art reflected her love of what was natural and part of the land; her gardening was organic because that was, at base, what all her life was about.

She never sought praise or applause. As Tim says, her modesty belied all those talents and capacities of hers: her guitar playing, her flower growing which calls to mind an anecdote related by Jenny, which is that her mother, when a very little girl, cut a flower out of *her* mother's dress to use as part of a pattern of her own making.

Perhaps it was anyway a pointer to her future work as a photographer when she experimented adventurously with her camera, as Becky describes it, using the camera with the Leica lens, trying to match what she saw through the viewfinder with what was in her imagination. And as for her painting, well Clem voices what others observed: that if she hadn't devoted her work to the service of other causes, she could have been a named artist in her own right.

By the late 1990s, Karen and Clem had decided to go their own ways; her work as a carer and as an art therapist was devouring all her time anyway. And her friendships took on strengths and character that filled and fulfilled her life. One was with Marianne, who continues her account of their long and close relationship with these memories:

"As the children grew older and they moved to 6 Long Meg Cottages, I have memories of Karen and her fairy tale sculptures; she learnt to weld and often used the workshop in Unthank to build her pieces: I had a garden open day and Karen arrived with a car full of sculptures of busts for which Jenny had been the model; she had to be cut out when the plaster set! We arranged the sculptures amongst the plants in my garden – it caused quite a stir on the fellside: the farmers loved them!

"In more recent years when Karen and I became even closer friends we used to go to the Sunday alternative cinema in Keswick, eating fish and chips out of newspaper, refusing to have polystyrene trays, in the market square. Our meetings were always full of banter and with Karen's sharp wit and increasing wisdom. Karen was a loving friend and also supportive of me, she taught me the value of quiet reflection and we shared a love of the celebration of ordinary things.

"My most vivid memory is on an evening in May, I cycled the seven miles to Little Salkeld from Unthank, we drank sambuca around the fire, laughed, a lot, and I set off in the dark. The May blossom was so white it lit the road and I got home and texted Karen to tell her about it, she replied, 'sweet dreams'.

"Karen believed fiercely and passionately in unconditional love and this kept her steadfast through difficult times. I think this was the essence of her work as an art therapist, her tender support of young people and as mother to her pride and joy: Jenny and Tim. Karen had to know that Jenny and Tim are strong and secure, she was incredibly proud of them. Together with Leon and Becky, they have become a force to be reckoned with."

Margaret Armstrong knew Karen from the early 1980s and recalls how forceful a member of the women's group she was and how naturally she applied herself and her skills to supporting women in need and discussing strategies for care and change. Margaret also has many memories of times less serious – like discovering that Karen could be quite prudish about the nude bathing on a Formentera beach during a holiday on Ibiza.

She also notes – as do many – how uncomplaining Karen was about the disease she knew would kill her. She wanted to go out, be with her friends, walk and talk, go for lunch at the George. She was dismissive of risk, ignoring the medics' instructions not to do anything too strenuous. But then, says Margaret, the oncologists were terrified of her. She even joked that the only sadness was that she probably wouldn't live to see the Royal Wedding!

Marion Smith, one of Karen's circle of closest friends, met her as a mature art student at college in Carlisle in the mid-1990s. She saw in Karen someone very clever, sensitive, a brilliant artist but first and foremost a caring, compassionate woman.

From her feminism to the wider issues of civil rights, Karen was an unswerving defender of those on the edge of society, and as the two became closer, Marion saw how amazing her friend was – "she could be hysterically funny and deadly serious in the same sentence." As an artist, she had the finest of artistic ideals but had her feet planted solidly on the ground. She relished the access the college gave her to a forge and the sculpture studio.

Karen Foulds

Another member of what they called the gang was Barbara, who is in New Zealand but who has put down some of her reminiscences in an email forwarded by Marion, who describes it as a shortlist of the only ones that are repeatable. They include the time they took the dogs up Dufton Pike and lay down and made snow angels – lovely, she notes "but lacking that vital edge."

Then there was the occasion when Karen was driving Barbara and their kids to Manchester Airport to go on holiday, and Barbara directed her on to the motorway but against the oncoming traffic. Barbara's contribution to the proceedings was to utter a very rude word – over and over and over again. Karen simply did a nippy about-turn, calmly saving the day and her passengers. The children eventually recovered, unlike Barbara.

'From her feminism to the wider issues of civil rights, Karen was an unswerving defender of those on the edge of society'

"The best is the famous Gate Incident. We were on our way back from a lovely couple of days at Portpatrick, and stopped to look at some standing stones. The area was fenced, and Barb and Annette weren't for climbing it, so they set about working out how to dismantle a bit of fence so they could get through. After quite a bit of huffing, puffing and swearing, they started to remove a fence panel from its posts.

"They were close to completing their task when Karen arrived, walked straight past them, opened the gate a couple of yards along the fence, and strolled on up to the stones. Not a word – just her best-ever use of the famous raised eyebrow. Mind you, we all know exactly what she was thinking."

Finally, we have a loving tribute from Anne-Lise, who knew Karen for 23 years. She writes this:

"Karen has left footprints in our hearts; quite literally concrete footprints to remember her by. She was a wonderfully inventive sculptress with an eye for the quirky and magical. Her sculptures were often born out of mythical creatures and from old fairytales or from vegetables she grew in her own garden. The makings of the sculptures took a lot of effort; working with iron and concrete takes blood, sweat and tears to bring them to life.

"In her art she was able to show her affection for others and those close to her knew how much work had gone into these creations. So many of us, her friends, have her sculptures dotted around our gardens. I am greeted every morning by her three pecking hens in the middle of the lawn. They are so lifelike that people coming to our house often comment that they didn't know we keep chickens. The chickens became so popular that Karen got fed up making them as she had so many other ideas to create in iron and concrete so the moulds were eventually broken.

"As you move around the garden you will find other hidden treasures, for instance a flying fish and plenty of gourds and pumpkins and a female torso. When visiting other friends of hers you can be sure to find plenty more of her sculptures gracing their gardens. They will always be a lovely reminder of the Karen we knew. We have her spirit living on in our gardens and houses as well as in our hearts.

"Karen was like a beautiful diamond locked in a box, difficult to get to but when you did you found a person with a loyal and generous nature unrivalled by any. I was honoured to be her friend."

Clem sums up his former partner simply: "An utterly Cumbrian woman, strong, determined, irrepressible, capable, accomplished, close to the landscape and the lore of the Lakes, the North Country from which she came."

The funeral ceremony for Karen Foulds was held at Penrith Cemetery Chapel and Beacon Edge Woodland on Friday March 18 2011

Leslie Halliman 1946-2011

J ust as he seldom if ever spoke maliciously or grudgingly of others, so it's impossible to find anyone who has anything but affection and esteem for Les Halliman. That's echoed in countless tributes that have appeared in cards, letters, phone calls and emails over these last few days. All speak of a man who had a limitless capacity for cheering people up, of adding value to their lives.

As a man he was generous, outgoing and companionable, attributes already visible in the boy growing up the quiet Tyneside suburb of Wrekenton. Les had arrived in the world in 1946, an only child to Rebecca and Henry Halliman – known to everyone as Bec and Henna. And Les was the apple of their eyes but never spoiled. He was a boy with boundless energy, fascinated by the world around him, innocently mischievous, bright as a button.

He played as a lad in the fields around Wrekenton, learned to swim, enjoyed family holidays staying in the caravan they had at the coast – got to know the beaches and the rocky shores from Newbiggin down to Whitburn and sometimes just went for days out with his mother, from whom he absorbed her compassionate nature and not a little wisdom too. It was a time when his cousin Malcolm and second cousin Keith formed their strong, close bonds with Les.

They were friends and family combined, and both speak of the young Les with warm memories of shared boyhoods – an era that would shape the links they maintained with one another for all of their lives. Keith recalls the nurturing in Les of a passion for fishing, which Henna passed on to the lad. First there was sea fishing and then, as time went by, the young ones taught themselves fly fishing, spending hours on the Coquet polishing their skills, relishing one another's company.

At the age of 12 or so, Les was already talking of what he wanted to be when he left school, where he'd been a reasonably diligent but never academically inclined pupil. His own dad worked as a maintenance painter at International Paints in Gateshead. Les wanted to be what his Uncle Johnny – Malcolm's father – was: a joiner, who was employed by the same firm. And that's what he did, signed up as an indentured apprentice and served his time with the company.

He was a model apprentice, worked hard in the job and studied without sparing himself both on day-release and night-school schemes. In later years, Les would look back with satisfaction on those years he spent acquiring knowledge and experience as an apprentice. Not an hour of the hard graft was wasted, for it conferred upon Les not only the practical competence he would deploy for the rest of his years but also a set of attitudes to life that, in their way, were priceless.

Before they were 18 and old enough to go where drink was served, Les and Malcolm used to frequent the long-gone, much-lamented Club A Gogo in Percy Street, Newcastle, and sit over soft drinks and coke in the Young Set room while they listened to stars of rock and roll, folk, and the blues – they saw Bo Diddley, Sonny Boy Williamson, the Rolling Stones, John Mayall and the Bluesbreakers – the best there were.

And as soon as they were old enough to buy pints of Ex, they crowded into the club's jazz lounge, where the bill might well include Dave Brubeck or any of a dozen top British jazz groups. The two young men were regulars, and it added to rather than replaced other pursuits that Les had followed – rugby among them. He just had so much energy for activities, which of course included fishing, with enough left over for some fairly vigorous parties.

But even then, Les seems to have developed the facility for simply going to sleep when he'd had enough. He could turn off as fast as a light switch, be jiving one minute and slumbering behind a settee the next. All of this – and the fishing – overlapped easily with the progress he was making in his work as a joiner. Getting a car had made a difference to the geography of his fishing. When he was seventeen, he had bought his first car, a Morris Minor. He and his dad hand-painted it.

It meant that Les could range much further afield – up to Rothbury and beyond to the Tweed, which became a favourite place. In his work, he had moved a couple of times, for a while with Kendal Cross and the contractors Brims. Then, at some point, in a life rooted in the North East and which looked likely to stay that way, Les decided to move hundreds of miles south.

Leslie Halliman

He had concluded that his future lay in being a clerk of works, saw an ad for an assistant at Basingstoke in Hampshire, and moved down, initially staying with Keith Marden, who was then working with the DSS as a civil servant. Les eventually found digs in the same house as a couple who became great friends – Janice and Phil. He was to be assistant clerk of works for three years after which he got a job, based in Dunstable in Bedfordshire, as full clerk for Brixton Estates.

While Les was there his mother, on holiday in Morecambe, died quite suddenly. That may or may not have been the trigger, but Les seems to have decided at that point to return to his native territory. He took a job on the Eldon Square development back in Newcastle and then with Ainsworth Spark, building stations and other structures on the Tyneside Metro network. But in July 1981, something happened that was far more important than all these career moves.

He went on holiday to Crete with Keith and friends. And just as their holiday was beginning, another was coming to an end for a group of two nurses and two midwives. They had two more days to spend on the island before going back to their jobs in the West Midlands. On the night of which we speak, the two groups of friends met and Les asked one of the midwives – Karen Thornicroft – for a dance. Les turned out to be a good dancer – "quite a mover", according to Karen.

Anyway, they danced most of that night away and after meeting by chance on the next day, they arranged to spend the following day – Karen's last of the holiday – together. Just the two of them. On parting, they promised they'd stay in touch, swapped phone numbers and addresses; Karen packed and, in the morning, left. Over the next week or so, back at home, she received a series of postcards, all bearing a single large letter. The first to arrive had just the letter E.

She thought this meant Ended, that their encounter was just a brief fling that this attractive man – this clerk of works – was signing off in a strange shorthand. But it was simpler and much better than that. The card she received was out of the order in which Les had sent them. The eight postcards with their eight letters had spelled out "I-l-o-v-e-y-o-u". Within three days, she had that worked out – and the best of it was that she felt exactly the same.

On the first weekend Les could get away after his holiday ended, he arranged to go to Birmingham to see Karen. Her mother – Rhoda – says she was so concerned by the original plan for Karen to travel north on her own to stay with Les that she insisted he first came down to their house in

Harborne so that she and John could see who it was their daughter was getting involved with. Not surprisingly, and more or less immediately, they liked and approved of the man they met that weekend.

Soon after that, Karen went to stay with Les in the house he'd saved up to buy in Thorpe Cottages, the old stone terrace in Ryton. With his professional skills and inventiveness, plus help from Keith, he was to restore and improve that place and turn it into a very comfortable home – which later was to be enlarged after buying the adjoining property and doing more work on the place. By then, Karen had moved permanently and had a job as a sister at Princess Mary's Maternity Hospital.

'Les's eight postcards spelled out "I-l-o-v-e-y-o-u". Within three days, Karen had that worked out, and the best of it was that she felt exactly the same'

In November 1985, Les and Karen were married in the Warwickshire village of Curdworth. It was a brilliant, lively day, a ceilidh band played, and Karen was surprised to find that they were off to the Gambia for their honeymoon. She had wanted to go to Florence and savour the beauty of its paintings, frescoes, architecture and music. Les had thought that swapping a British winter for West African warmth made sense.

And he would make a joke while they were there that she'd always remember. Looking out from the veranda of the house where they were staying, he said - with false portentousness - "It's a jungle out there, you know..." The following year, Karen found she was expecting a baby, and a son Laurie was born, at which point she gave up work for a while, then resumed until after a second child, Annie, was born in 1989.

Princess Mary's sadly closed in 1993: Karen's happy memories of the place when she worked there chime with equally good recollections of what life was like for her and Les after they settled as a couple. He had more job changes, including, briefly, a spell in the architects' department of NatWest Bank, where they suggested that it might be a good career move for him were he to join the Freemasons. He didn't think so – and left.

By now, Les was a very experienced professional, versed not only in the physical and technical aspects of building development, but in the social and economic environment. So his next job stop, with Enterprise 5, the housing association, was a logical move as was, even more so, the move to

Leslie Halliman

Municipal Mutual as a site surveyor a year or two later. Not long after that, the firm was taken over by the financial giant Zurich.

This was to be Les's employer until his retirement and - through his experience, his professionalism, his loyalty and his hard work - he must have been one of the company's greatest assets. He worked largely from home, but travelled vast distances throughout northern England as a face of Zurich: Keith thinks he was driving 50,000 miles a year at the height of this period. And, increasingly, he was doing business in Cumbria.

What more natural, then, than to move to the county in which he spent so much time and to which he was increasingly drawn because of its natural beauty. And making a new start there was to put down roots that would be fresh for him, for Karen and for the children. So they moved to Carlisle, making their home in Holly House, the Courtyards, at Moorhouse for eleven happy and eventful years. Laurie and Annie have vivid memories of that period in their lives.

He played out with the children, encouraged, you might even say challenged them to be adventurous and imaginative, filled their lives with doing things from blackberrying to helping him build and then occupying the tree house, to jumping across streams and becks, scrambling up slopes and over beaches at Rockcliffe and Kipford, running and swimming. He was unstoppable – and expected them to be too. He called Annie his little mountain goat: you get the picture.

As well as that, he read to them, giving them lifts everywhere when they were at school. He was the best sort of dad imaginable, much more like a pal than a parent. At home, life was good too. Karen had taken a job at Laura Ashley – a break from midwifery simply to be busy and earn an income; Les was as attentive to detail as ever in his job with Zurich.

Then, about 15 years ago, he was diagnosed with diabetes and, rather than slow down, he discovered walking – in fact it was almost as though Les Halliman was the original walker. Increasingly, it was an activity that drew on all his qualities – especially the painstaking way in which he'd read about and research every walk.

And those walks became more and more demanding. He read every Wainwright from title page to the last full point. He learned and honed a knowledge of the countryside, especially the fells, that vied with that of the great Wainwright himself and, as Malcolm says, when Les took up walking he soon was insisting that everyone took up walking. One by one, his friends joined him in completing successive walks; in turn, the walks brought him new friends.

Les kept a logbook of his walks, from leisurely rambles to an ascent of Ben Nevis, a veritable testament to his thoroughness, his enthusiasm, his humanity. It begins with helpful notes about how each walk should be tackled and what to do in any situation; carries details about car registration and mobile phone numbers, last-minute changes and so on – and then records some of the countless walks he led or suggested. One, six years ago, is referred to as "Claire's birthday walk" or Clairathon.

His log reports how "the whole gang walked up the back of Ullswater from Patterdale car park to How Tarn, where we got the ferry back. The weather was good, sunny, clear with a light breeze, ideal conditions. I think everybody enjoyed the day. This is a smashing walk, easy on the feet and legs, not too many hills, lots to watch on the water and plenty of stopping places."

'Les read every Wainwright from title page to the last full point. He learned and honed a knowledge of the fells that vied with the great Wainwright himself'

Others were far more challenging. One, captured in a photo that's particularly arresting, has him on a mountainside and almost covered in snow, gale-blown and barely recognisable as a human being save for glimpses of the red clothing beneath the white. It's images like these that will stay in the minds of his friends – and images of his days out fishing, which again played a big part in his life as early retirement from Zurich beckoned.

Not that there was much retiring. That wasn't really a word you'd find in his lexicon. On top of work, walking, and fishing, Les had decided as the twentieth century drew to a close that it was time to build a new house. Literally. He and Karen acquired a plot at Marsh House Gardens, he drew up the plans, and he constructed Number Seven himself as far as building regulations would allow.

It is, as you all know, a wonderful house, and speaks of the happiness they knew as a family and the hard work and talent Les embodied. But there was so much of that in Holly House too, where Les and Karen made such firm friends with their neighbours Stephen and Jane. Stephen was one of those was recruited into Les's enthusiasms, learned fishing, went on walks, grew to know and respect and love this extraordinary man.

He was among those who accompanied Les on the banks of the Tweed,

Leslie Halliman

the Allen, the Eden, who learned about countryside he'd never really known about, became aware that Les knew every fell by name and shape, laughs as he remembers that Les took their dog for walks that even tired out the dog. And Les walked everywhere, abroad as well as in the Lakes, the Yorkshire Dales, the Peak District – he was extremely knowledgeable about them all.

He was to involve children too – children who hadn't previously enjoyed the chance to get out and doing anything creative or adventurous. Working with another Clare, he would take youngsters from St Bedes into the Lakes. Both he and the children got so much out of these trips. And it underlined the fact that children were naturally drawn to this man: he was one of those adults who can enter the world of the child and be accepted.

Over this period, of course, we are skipping much else in Les's life. Laurie and Annie grew up, Annie later going to Loughborough to read sociology. She graduated just over a week ago – and Les knew that she'd got her degree, for the news was texted to him during his last walk along the Pennine Way. Karen had taken up – brilliantly – her work as a special-needs assistant working for Cumbria County Council and then, nine years ago, had resumed her midwifery.

We are at risk both of leaving out too much from the life story we have come to celebrate and of putting in so much as to make it indigestibly complete, for Les packed in more to his life than most who live decades longer. He never wasted time or his own potential. Talking to his mother-in-law Rhoda, who was so close and who accompanied him often on local walks, you learn that he took courses in tiling and plumbing after Zurich and deployed those skills generously. He was a great comfort to Rhoda when she lost John.

We have almost overlooked the important part played by Ann, who shared a lot of her childhood with Les. She was orphaned aged only eight when her mum died and she was taken in by Les's mum Bec. She has many happy memories of that time and after she married and had her own children. At one point, being quite a bit older than Les, she did his washing and cooked his tea when Henna and Bec were on holiday.

She tells of how Les went bald when he was in his twenties and used to sport a Bobby Charlton style comb-over for some years until he finally asked her trim it for him, which revealed his bald head for all to see. Her sons Ian and Colin spent time helping Les with renovating that first house in Ryton when they were young men. So many poignant memories.

Les's wife Karen has the final word:

"When I look around our home, there are so many reminders of Les's talents, especially in the carpentry department. He worked so hard to build us all a beautiful home and we were so proud of what he had achieved.

"One of the things I loved about Les was his knowledge of geography and nature, he always used to know the name of a mountain or type of bird. It was very reassuring to have him lead a walk, and I always felt very safe at his side.

"Les will never see the marriages of our children or the birth of our grandchildren. He was always so good with babies and children, as many of you will know.

"Les was a man of simple needs, who had a good heart, and was the most sociable of men who believed in living life to the full.

"Seeing you all here makes me very proud that he was mine. The thirty years that he was part of my life were an adventure...and I wouldn't have missed it for the world."

The funeral ceremony for Leslie Halliman was held at Carlisle Crematorium on Friday July 26 2011

Deborah Sue Godsey 1951-2012

Deborah Sue Godsey – Debbie Sue – was one of four children born to Hugh and Hester Godsey and brought up in Lynchburg, Virginia, after a spell in nearby Richmond. Little Debbie was exactly that – so little and only three pounds in weight when she was born three months prematurely that her wrists were too small to carry an identity tag. Transcending such a precarious beginning is possibly why she became so resolutely full of life.

Indeed, her sister Pat tells of how the family used to say no one would have bet a nickel on her survival at the outset but that when she was seven or so and Debbie five she remembers a younger sister who was so energetic, so active, so determined to make every minute count. In appearance she was a blond angel with curly hair belying her slightly tomboy inclinations to ride the horse and ponies in which her dad made a supplementary living as a trader.

Surrounding their suburban Lynchburg home was space – space to ride and exercise the horses and ponies, room for the girls, and later a boy, a succession of much-loved dogs, a backyard big enough to grow the plants and vegetables that became so much a part of Debbie's fascination for the natural botanical, horticultural world; and wildlife in abundance. Debbie's horizons expanded, her interests waxed, and by the time her young sister Cindy was old enough to recall what Debbie was like those recollections are of a wise and caring older sister.

Debbie, she says, was always helpful, protective, communicative, knew about the world they inhabited – and not a little about the world they would inhabit. Her practical talents by then were such that she could help construct dolls' houses for Cindy, furnish and adorn them using outstanding dressmaking skills and a knowledge of fabrics and other materials; there was also her wise counsel as their childhoods turned into teenage.

"Learn to cook before you get out of the house" was her advice, and – probably most telling – "Listen to all the others' opinions, then make up your own mind." By the mid-to-late 1960s, it was counsel that had a special resonance. Civil rights had been secured – technically – but the Godseys were surrounded by communities where legislation had made little impact on prejudice. Debbie was listening to Simon and Garfunkel (underrated even today as protest singers) to Joan Baez and Joni Mitchell; she was seeing Martin Luther King and reading Norman Mailer.

Debbie had passed through her teenage years with grace and quiet confidence, doing well at E C Glass High School, where her open-minded

and intellectually adventurous outlook seems to have sat easily alongside the formal class style of the school. She left to take a college course as a trainee teacher, and later to study briefly as a possible social worker; neither of those ambitions was pursued. Instead, Debbie went to nursing school, following the steps of her mother and her sister Pat.

She prospered on the two-year degree course and was soon working in Baltimore as a general nurse, then in ICU at the University of Virginia Hospital, where Pat was, at one point, technically her boss.

Pat was once obliged to tell her otherwise conscientious but impetuous younger sister that you couldn't take a two-hour lunch to discuss and develop some other project, however worthwhile. But Debbie was like that, which explains why she almost always worked part time: her other activities and interests were too important – and they really were – to be fettered by conventional timetables and divisions of life into work and recreation. She didn't recognise that sort of barrier.

Deborah Sue Godsey

By then, she was working nights in a renal unit, developing expertise that would be highly prized, but she saw it is as simply a part of her life, not its totality. She had also found a house that suited her wonderfully. Not too far from the hospital in Charlottesville, Land's End Cottage seemed like miles from anywhere; no other houses were visible; there were fields and woods, cattle on farmland. It was idyllic.

It so happened that, studying for a postgraduate degree in maths at the University of Virginia, was a young and very talented mature student. Michael Dritschel, looking for accommodation, saw rooms advertised in a house not far away. It was Land's End Cottage. But after Debbie agreed following an interview to let to him, she told her friend Janice she was having second thoughts; she wasn't sure they could get on.

They got on. And they stayed at Land's End Cottage for seven years, during which time Debbie became a nursing specialist in the field of renal care and dialysis; Michael honed and polished his expertise as a mathematician. They also passed to one another a panoply of interests.

'For Debbie, activities and interests were too important to be fettered by conventional timetables and divisions of life into work and recreation'

Debbie had started a goat dairy in the early stages of being at Land's End. She had a Toggenburg and two Nubians; later she was to acquire a Mohair and a spinning wheel to make the yarn. As one of her sisters says, Debbie's attitude was "if you want some wool, first get a sheep." It never went to that, and the spinning wheel didn't get pressed into permanent service, but you know what they meant. Debbie was never the consumer, buying other people's manufacture – and the mediocrity that so often went with it. She followed all that was natural and which took honest effort in its production.

She was a great believer in home and everything that went with the concept, and seems to have espoused some of the Amish concepts of self-sufficiency. She described herself to at least one of her Hexham friends as "a home bird", which you knew didn't mean someone who sat indoors and watched tv, for she and Michael have been among those brave few who have managed to convince the licensing authority that they don't have a television receiver.

So Land's End Cottage was the base for outside work, but was also where goats and kids were reared, fed, and milked on the paddock or in the shed that served as a parlour; where food was painstakingly grown; where cooking paid due tribute to the gardening that sent as much as possible from tilth to table. It was a paradigm of conservation and commonsense; and, through it all, Michael learned constantly from Debbie. It was where Debbie first kept bees. She went to see an old man who was disposing of two hives of bees. Holding up a piece of equipment he told Debbie the price: $10. She looked uncertain until he made it plain that was what he was asking for the whole lot – equipment, hives, and the colony. She bought it all, and kept it for six years.

It was, says Pat, something she did for the joy of doing it properly. She never cut corners, never did anything less than whole-heartedly, and the bees episode was par for her course. Everything she did was enveloped in the cheerfulness, the optimism, the laughter that were all part of her signature.

She grew in self-assurance from the somewhat shy young woman Michael had first met. Her cultural and political values were solidifying, allying herself on a wing that was certainly well to the left by American standards but was personal rather than institutional. Debbie knew what she believed in; didn't need a movement to belong to. By the time they left Land's End Cottage she was 38, and Michael had just got an assistant professorship at Purdue, Indiana.

She was working at Home Hospital in Lafayette when they moved to an isolated farmhouse known not by a name but only by a postal address that measured the miles it was located from the county courthouse. There was a lot of work to do, fixing up the house: the previous owner, an elderly woman, had not used the upstairs part of the place for years. It was lost in the middle of fields of windswept corn and soya bean.

Anyone who has seen Michael's extraordinary skills as a carpenter should know that this was also where those skills began to develop. And Debbie worked alongside him: days spent dialysing kidney patients gave way to evenings rubbing down and sanding woodwork, painting, and wallpapering. The smallholding they had was located on good soil for growing vegetables. Debbie gardened prodigiously hard; they ate well.

In 1991, by now living in another place, this one an Indiana farmhouse, they were married in their garden by a Justice of the Peace. There was a small gathering – the four parents and Cindy's son Justin, who'd been warned that the ceremony was taking place

Deborah Sue Godsey

on yet another construction site and that he'd better wear a hard hat.

Michael took a year out in a job at a university in Northern Holland. Researching and teaching maths to Dutch students was a satisfying alternative to working on a not always appreciative Mid-West campus. On his return, Michael's temporary job moves dictated where he and Debbie would live – Williamsburg, North Carolina, then Charlottesville again, followed by another spell at Purdue. Debbie moved, dialysed at various hospitals, gardened, kept home.

By the late 1990s, Michael and Debbie were familiar with Europe; academic work had taken him to more than one country, and they had both visited the UK to call on his brother David in Cambridge and then in St Andrew's, Scotland.

On one journey north they'd passed through Corbridge and remembered how attractive a county Northumberland was. In 1999, when Newcastle University invited Michael for interview, his response – and Debbie's – was immediate and positive. He was offered a permanent teaching and research post, and in September 1999 moved to England. Debbie packed up and stayed to supervise their house sale, enduring a tornado in the weeks that intervened. Fortunately insurance covered the cost of repairing the limited damage, and the ongoing sale wasn't threatened.

Michael had stayed at first with friends Andrew and Cathy Duncan at Oakwood before finding an apartment in St Mary's Chare. Then Debbie arrived in November, closely followed by furniture, belongings, and dogs Lucy and Zeno, who had to spend six months in the Netherlands getting their initial passports but who lived on until a year or so ago. Soon they were all in the house on Park Avenue.

The house was perfect for them – perfectly habitable but with the scope for the restoration and improvements that they wanted to make. The garden was interesting, extensive, attractive, though soil and weather conditions took all of Debbie's painstaking flexibility and understanding to control. They bought the property on what must have seemed to Americans an odd basis – the sealed bid, which was then still quite common in the North East.

In the meantime, they had new jobs to take up. In Michael's case it was as a lecturer, later promoted to reader, in maths at Newcastle; and Debbie eventually at Hexham Hospital, for which she was able to transfer her US nursing licence. She found the work hard and was paid around a quarter of what she could earn in the US. In fact she went back there on more than one occasion to do some temporary work in Virginia and save a little cash to help pay for the work they were doing on Park Avenue.

After realising that the hours weren't compatible with public transport to work in a Newcastle hospital Debbie started to care for an ailing neighbour, Lorna. This took up more and more of her time; eventually, Debbie became a carer for Northumberland County Council, work she did until just after Lorna's death in 2011. She got to know the county well, having acquired a driving licence by then, and made many firm friends among her clients.

It was less so with those in charge of the system, for whom Debbie had little more time than she'd had for senior management in similar organisations back home. A familiar story, it seems, wherever care is administered by pie-chartists and box tickers. But the consolations for Debbie, just as in her previous life, were her gardening, her cooking and baking, her dogs, her care for home and for nature. And music, again, played a part in her life.

'She found hospital work hard and was paid around a quarter of what she could earn in the US. She returned to Virginia for temporary work to pay for improvements in Hexham'

In her youth, she had learned to play the piano and had also picked up the guitar. In Hexham, she learned the ukulele too. Her choice in music was the down to earth and the demotic: she enjoyed folk and popular music; classical formed a background to these; and she shared, though not always with the same degree of enthusiasm, Michael's love of contemporary jazz.

Debbie's sisters also have abiding memories of her. Cindy, staying in Hexham last year, went with her sister to Beamish, to York, to castles in Northumberland. "She was fun, she was cheerful, there was the old laughter." It was, Debbie had said, "the best visit ever from the US," and they shared another happy and hilarious memory: of her making Cindy some underclothes – pantaloons and camisole in a fabric patterned in eighteenth century style. Beautiful, but about five times over size, and they were still laughing about that.

Pat remembers the donkey their father bought – called Lorraine, it was much loved by them all but especially by Debbie. And she remembers that Debbie made everything if she possibly could: "If she wanted English muffins back in the States, well she made English muffins." Cindy talks of her making pasta from scratch. There weren't many packets and cans in Debbie's larder.

Two of Debbie's closest family couldn't be here today. Her dad, Hugh, and her brother Mike. Talking on the phone yesterday, Hugh had this to say: "She was a wonderful child – all her life – inside and out. Naturally very clever, always there when you wanted her. She'll be so sorely missed. I'm just as sick as a mule..."

We also heard by email from Debbie's brother Mike. He and his wife Teresa are holding a simple ceremony in Lynchburg to coincide with this one. He had this to say: "Debbie was a special person, someone with a sense of empathy and justice. She was a loving sister – always – and when I behaved badly and irresponsibly as a youngster, she would often deflect blame onto herself. Debbie loved me, and I adored her – and always will."

Finally, we are to hear from the one who has shared so much of Debbie's life and been as close as any human being could be. Michael Dritschel, Debbie's lover, her husband, her carer, her friend.

"I miss her terribly – her company, her love, her keen intelligence and extraordinary talents, the things we shared from cooking to gardening to mushroom collecting to music. She was someone I could commiserate with in the trials of being a stranger in a foreign culture, as well as feeling sometimes that being here was like being permanently on holiday. It feels as if half of me is missing."

The funeral ceremony for Deborah Sue Godsey was held St Andrew's Chapel and the Woodland Burial Ground, Hexham, on Friday January 27 2012

Hetty Baron-Thieme   1930-2012

Hetty came into the world in 1930, one of four children born to a Dutch mother, Ans, and German father, Johann Gottfried Thieme. She was brought up initially in Java, where her father was a scientist working on plantations established by Dutch settlers producing chocolate, coffee, and rubber. The German branch of Hetty's family had literary as well as scientific provenance: her grandfather, a journalist, had written a best-selling novel about the Thirty Years War.

It was a happy colonial childhood, with all the privileges and diversions you'd expect: many years later, Hetty was to describe hers as "an affectionate and demonstrative" family. It could have been an idyll lasting for the rest of her young life but was, instead, suddenly, dramatically, terribly transformed. Their experiences after the German Army invaded Holland in 1940, with the consequent repercussions on Dutch overseas territories, followed by the Japanese assault on South-east Asia, involved Hetty and her family in a long and challenging odyssey.

In post-war Europe, Hetty eventually came from Holland, where she'd been at convent school in Romond, to England and a teacher training course at Digby Stuart College, now part of the University of Roehampton, an elevation that would have amused Hetty, who had been told by her mother that a teaching diploma was quite sufficient for a girl who would anyway be getting married.

In notes she made at a much later stage of life, Hetty recalled that teaching itself was not satisfying; there was rarely time to devote to those pupils she felt most needed her attention. She much preferred – and discovered a knack for – helping so-called difficult children. She worked in schools where such children were numerous, and in one school was put in charge of ten deprived youngsters, using relatively new techniques in social education.

On a walking holiday she had met Adrian Fuller, an architect, and married him in 1953, the year she started working, first as a nursery teacher, in East London schools. A daughter Hellie was born in 1954, followed by a son Jan, and then another girl, Phoebe, both born after Hetty and Adrian had moved, through his work, to live in the East Midlands.

It was not an untroubled marriage. Hetty, concerned by her husband's emotional state, developed her knowledge and insight into family instability and how, in her words, "something positive can be gained from all life experiences, including the difficult ones." She helped to set up a group for lonely and housebound wives – a group that met monthly over many years – and she was involved with and trained in group therapy by the newly-founded Marriage Guidance Council.

'Hetty's career as a social worker was marked by acute comprehension of people's problems and by commitment to those in her care'

As marital isolation ensued, and now back in London, Hetty had the house enlarged to set up a playgroup, an activity which she and others saw as a vital but missing link in family development, and she was to become a founder member of the Pre-school Playgroups Association. Following her divorce in 1972, she was accepted on a diploma course in social work at the London School of Economics. Hetty had been traumatised by the marital collapse but had tremendous resilience and steadily rebuilt her life.

Hetty's career as a social worker was marked by her acute comprehension of people's problems and by an inordinate commitment to those in her care, qualities we'll hear spelled out more fully in a few minutes by one of her great friends and former colleague. Meanwhile, Hetty was bringing up a family on her own, and they recall a mother who seems to have been more like a pal than a parent. Hellie describes how her world revolved round her mother.

"She was a great and adventurous cook, she ground the beans for coffee, cared for the garden with enthusiasm and proficiency, adored wildlife." Hetty went hedgehog-hunting and made a record of their trails and tracks, eventually mapping out the territory for a whole community of the creatures. Mealtimes included stories about Hetty's childhood; she would talk sometimes in Dutch – and pass on pieces of that language to the children.

It was, says Hellie, "a rich childhood for us." Hetty had learned to play the guitar and the violin as a child; she shared her musical inclinations with her own youngsters; at one time Hellie played piano, her brother Jan the viola, and Phoebe the violin – a quartet that, on a few occasions, entertained other family members and friends.

Phoebe, four years younger than her sister, has images of her mother listening to Radio 3. "She was a morning person – always full of ideas and enthusiasm," though there could also be quiet times as Hetty slowly reinvented herself. Eventually she was to enter into a new, strong and enduring relationship that came about partly through Phoebe herself. She had a friend at Surbiton High – Joanna Baron – whose father Michael met Hetty on one of the girls' visits to each other's home.

It was, if not love at first sight, something of strength and growing intensity as Hetty and Michael, then a lawyer practising in Twickenham, got to know one another. They shared many interests – music, the arts, social issues, the outdoors. "We had a lot in common," says Michael, "and soon meant a lot to one another." Michael moved in with Hetty in the late 1970s, and later they bought the flat in Archer House, Battersea. That was in 1981, by which time Hetty had become a very experienced social worker.

Gillian Ruch, now Gillian Broad, joined Wandsworth Council as a newly-qualified social worker in 1985. Hetty is remembered by her as "an untypical manager in some respects – frequently arriving at work with a wicker basket full of delicious food for everyone to share." Hetty was, says Gillian, "a professional mother, and the image of her with that basket makes me think of a mother hen nurturing, supporting, and protecting her young." The team's work was concentrated in the Southfields area of South London.

It involved many families and older people with mental health difficulties and disabilities. "Hetty's style was direct and uncomplicated," says Gillian: "she had a deep commitment to improving the lives of vulnerable people."

Hetty Baron-Thieme

As a supervisor, she was encouraging and dependable "if not at times a little intimidating, with her hand gestures and European accent." In this work, as in all the other activities to which she applied herself, Hetty never did things by halves.

Both Hellie and Phoebe tell of the care their mother would put into answering their questions fully, and – if she didn't know the answer – finding out what it was they wanted to know. She was a natural researcher, a careful note-taker, a diarist and a keeper of journals: that mattered even more when she and Michael moved to live at Loweswater and Hetty kept a meticulous and regular written record of all the wildlife she saw from Watergate Barn.

They had moved there after two years enjoying Thames-side life in West London but being increasingly drawn to the Lakes, where they loved to walk. Having briefly considered moving to the Quantocks, they settled on Watergate and never regretted it. It overlapped and encompassed a range of travel throughout their years together that reads like a world gazetteer: they went to Greece, India, Africa, the US, Portugal, Spain, Holland, Denmark, Hungary, the Galapagos Islands...

'She became a well-informed and influential figure in the world of bats – was very happy to be called "the batty lady" as a licensed bat worker with English Nature'

They walked and trekked, explored and made friendships, echoed and amplified Hetty's love of learning and of the world around her. It was something, much earlier on in her life, that had been reflected in journeys remembered by Hellie and Phoebe, who recall holidays in a Renault 4, when all five members of the family would squeeze in and drive down to Menton and – on one occasion – Rome. Back in Loweswater, Watergate became a hub for happy family gatherings.

Michael had sold his practice in the South and took factotum work in Whitehaven; Hetty turned from social work to issues that mattered more and more to her as time went by. She campaigned with Friends of the Earth, did an OU degree in Environmental Studies and Third World Development, securing a BA in 1995, and became a well-informed and influential figure in the world of bats – was very happy to be called "the batty lady".

Her bat studies formed part of the Field Studies Council's work on the subject; she was a licensed bat worker with English Nature, and gave talks to school and other groups throughout the western Lakes. Marvellously in tandem with this work of Hetty's was Michael's production of an anthology of poetry devoted to the creature, "On a Bat's Wing." Then, as if this and their travel didn't devour enough of their time and energy, there was Hetty's major contribution to the region's oral history project.

She recorded interviews with people throughout the Derwent and Lorton Fells History area, work which became a part of the Ambleside Oral History record. How did Hetty fit this in with a life that also included her striking embroidery of Loweswater scenes, her cooking and baking, her setting up of a food cooperative? Or her sailing the dinghy, which she shared so joyfully with the grandchildren, who she'd join when they took off to build dams and light fires?

Michael's frequent visitors, poets and writers who'd come to stay with him and speak at local gatherings, found themselves the beneficiaries of rare hospitality when they came to Watergate or, when in 2008 Michael and Hetty moved to South Street, Cockermouth.

However short the notice, soup would be made from tasty ingredients, fresh towels would be laid out by a comfortable bed, the welcome would be as genuine as the food.

Gillian Broad, whose fond memories of working with Hetty we heard earlier, stayed in touch and became a visitor to Loweswater. Here, she says, she saw Hetty "exhibiting her flair for design and detail in the construction and decoration of her home. Her love of bats and commitment to collecting the oral histories of native Cumbrians mirrored the qualities she displayed in her professional life – an interest in protecting and supporting less-well-recognised groups and those whose voices are not always heard."

Gillian concludes with a haiku she has written for a very special friend and colleague:

Sharp glance, with bent knee
Expressive fingers, nurture love
Tough, gentle Hetty

There are sure to be many other stories, other chapters, numerous episodes in Hetty's life that we risk having overlooked today. Among many messages of condolence, for instance, is this from Michael's niece Tasha in Noto, Sicily:

"I write from Bombello, under a new moon, where I see Hetty hand-in-hand with you, bringing her joyful, wide-eyed enthusiasm for this wild place; night skies; fruits of the forest, owls and other birdsong ...I know how challenging these last months have been for you, and while all will speak of her release from suffering, that doesn't lessen the loss to you of such a wonderful person and companion."

Then there's this message from Hetty's brother Gottfried – known as Fried and now living in the South of France – which says:

"I have so many lovely childhood memories of Hetty and had always looked up to her. As a youngster, she had taken me under her wing and cared for me. Not much later, I and my young family always stayed with her in England on our trips to Europe."

Michael's daughter Saskia says this: "we should remember how very, very happy Hetty and my father were together and how lovely that was to observe. Theirs was a great love affair, which lasted over forty years, and it always gave me hope that people could find their perfect partner, someone with whom they could share their passions, but who would also give them space to pursue their own interests.

"Hetty was always kind and thoughtful to me as a stepdaughter, supportive and wise, but never assumed the role of a mother. We had an uncomplicated love, and I feel very, very lucky to have had her in my life. Jacob, her step-grandson always loved spending time with Hetty too; she had infinite patience with him, teaching him how to play dominoes one rainy afternoon, and embarking on endless games of I Spy on long drives; he too will miss her very much."

No doubt the same applies to Jan's boys Sebastian and Luke. Saskia also writes of her brother Timothy: "Hetty was always immensely kind and loving towards him, taking Timothy into her life when she took Michael, a founder member of the National Autistic Society, as her husband. Timothy was always very happy going out on the lake in Hetty's rowing boat, and he relished his holidays with Michael and her. She was a wonderful stepmother to him and made him feel welcome and loved."

We can never lose the memories of anything that is good. The qualities that you loved in Hetty: her enthusiasms; her constructive, creative wisdom; her friendship and loyalty; her idealism and compassion; her strength and decency; and above all the love she had for her family, these qualities will never be lost.

Michael's other daughter Joanna has written her stepmother a poem for this occasion:

"We have shared so many good times you and I
trailing up fells, Michael striding ahead
Holding hands to help each other when the ground
Slip-slid precariously under us.

" You called me into the garden to show
the dark wings of a fallen peregine
stretched gently out in your hands;
we watched Mark part long grass
to reveal a pair of baby leverets waiting quietly in a scrape;
ate noisy sandwiches in our anoraks in bird-hides,
collected sea-tumbled pebbles
celebrated birthdays and holidays.

" We sat on your bed not so long ago and I told
you that you were the best step-mother in the world.
You laughed and said
'That's overdoing it a bit'

" What will remain of us is love
And love is all I know in my heart for you"

The funeral ceremony for Hetty Baron-Thieme was held at the Meadow Burial Ground,
Cockermouth, on Monday June 25 2012

Charles Bray

Charles Bray was known to some as Chas and others as Charlie, which is the name I'll use. Charlie grew up in the back streets of Salford, an only son to Charles and Minnie Bray. His father worked for the mill that produced Hovis flour; his mother had musical inclinations; her mother had been a famous singer in Wales. Charlie's grandfather had been an engine driver.

They weren't easy times: the streets in which the Brays lived were exactly those immortalised by Robert Roberts in his book about that part of Salford, "The Classic Slum." Charlie was the last pupil at his junior school to go there wearing clogs. But he seems to have been immune to privations and clearly focused his energies on getting everything possible out of the hours of the day.

Some of you will know that Charlie wrote his memoir, recording in great detail the events of his life. It is an extraordinarily literate, observant, insightful chronicle of his boyhood, documenting a time and a place suspended between Edwardian and modern life in the industrial North of England, a fine read filled with images of the factories, streets and shops, the buildings, the cinemas and theatres, and the individuals who populated his life.

He describes the human wealth of a community in which his own family was deeply embedded, with relatives living or working nearby and all with a deep sense of location, of belonging. And it was an environment in which his eventual love and grasp of both the arts and the sciences would be nourished. Listening to music, learning the piano, going into Peel Park museum and art gallery, he was also at ease with the industries and technologies that were the neighbourhood's lifeblood.

He was to become one of a rare breed of men and women who are at home in what C.P. Snow called The Two Cultures, traditionally and unbridgeably separated, and distanced even more by our educational system. Those like Charlie, who bestrode the two cultures, were just as informed about science and technology as about the arts and humanities. He became a true polymath. How this happened is easily traced back to what he did and what he was exposed to as a young boy.

He wandered on foot – and later by bicycle – all over his part of the industrial heartland, exploring the factories and the interconnected network of railways, rivers and canals that crisscrossed the North West. He grew to love good brass bands, the sort that enlivened the annual Whit Walks, and he played piano in public at the age of about 12.

He was a talented and clever boy – but it was natural wisdom, not the

examinable knowledge of the classroom. Thus, from his primary school, the grandly-named Windsor Institute, he failed to pass what in those pre-11+ days was called the scholarship, and went to the secondary school at Halton Bank, which he left, with few formal qualifications, at the tender age of 14. School-holiday and weekend jobs had familiarised him with aspects of industry – including a spell at the mill for which his father drove a wagon. His first real job was with a wholesale tools supplier in Shudehill.
This key part of the city centre bustled with small businesses servicing the great mercantile infrastructure of Manchester. Soon, Charlie joined a firm which made office furniture to exceptionally high standards. It was where Charlie learned not only the use of hand and machine tools, but where he acquired an understanding of the various woods and veneers, jointing techniques, glues and varnishes used in fine commercial cabinet-making.

He moved to become an apprentice with John Gough, another specialist joinery firm which fitted out ecclesiastical and public buildings. Charlie had clear recollections of working on beautifully-crafted pews, cupboards, shelving and counters in churches, convents, banks and libraries. Not only was he assembling a peerless knowledge of the arts and crafts involved but a familiarity with the social settings in which all these projects were ordered and completed. Then, at the age of 17, Charlie went to work for a while at the same mill where his father was employed – the Hovis plant beside the Manchester Ship Canal.

Just as he was becoming familiar with the intricate operation of the mill, the Second World War began to loom over everyone's lives. He joined the Home Guard, which he said was just like its caricature in "Dad's Army." Soon afterwards he enlisted in the Royal Navy.

Charles Bray

That was in preference to joining the Army, which he thought might involve him in personal combat, an intolerable prospect. His Navy career, extensive and colourful, took him from basic training in Suffolk to Devonport, and then to Bermuda, Scotland, Canada, the Caribbean, the US, Uruguay, Brazil and Ecuador. He went to the Galapagos Islands, to Peru and Chile, back to the UK via West Africa, and then on to the Far East via the Med and the Suez Canal.

Charlie was on HMS Rodney when the Bismarck was famously sunk, witnessed the scuttling of the Graf Spee in Montevideo, and served briefly on the ship that eventually carried the atom bomb detonated at Bikini Atoll. By then, Charlie had painted his first really serious picture – a portrait of an Indonesian nurse. He had bought paints and brushes while in Australia and always considered this a seminal point of his artistic career.

But he wasn't even half way through his twenties at this juncture: by the time he was demobbed in late 1945, Charlie Bray had packed more into his life than most people would do in their allotted span. He returned to Britain to pick up the threads of a civilian life in carpentry and joinery, but for Charlie – probably unsettled by the extraordinary events of his previous five or six years – the work lost its appeal.

Instead, he was accepted on an emergency teacher training course and began his studies and practical sessions at Freckleton College on the Fylde, between Preston and Blackpool. A fellow trainee, who went on to be the choirmaster at Liverpool Cathedral and knew of Charlie's musical talents, nearly persuaded him to apply for a place at the Royal College of Music – but that was a strand in Charlie's story that was left tantalisingly loose.

He persevered with the course and taught for a while in a Salford school before teaching woodwork and technical drawing to disadvantaged and disabled pupils in two nearby schools at Styal, then a sleepy Cheshire village just south of Manchester. There were two other schools – in the Beswick or Bradford districts of Manchester by the sound of them – which Charlie found daunting but which all added to the experience he was compiling.

In the evenings he was completing his City and Guilds of London Institute examinations and then attended Manchester Regional College of Art for life classes. Later that year – it would be 1949 or 1950 – he applied to study music at Goldsmiths College in London. Once there, he switched to an art course. This, remember, is the man who failed to get to grammar school.

Charlie had been involved with the scouting movement from his early teenage years, and had met scouts overseas during his war service in the

Far East. At home, he had close friends – who remained close for the rest of their lives – men like Vin Craven, with whom he shared the ideals and ideas of Baden Powell, and who also had wider outdoors interests.

In Derbyshire and the Lake District they rambled and camped. They climbed fells. They even went caving – an esoteric activity for many, but one that clearly engaged the young Charlie Bray, who could remember descending into Giant's Hole, near Winnats Pass at Castleton and the limestone caves in southern France and the Pyrenees.

After completing his studies at Goldsmiths, Charlie returned to the North and, for a while, worked in large secondary school in south Manchester – Wythenshawe by the sound of it. It was on a large estate not far from what would become today's international airport. Anyway, he soon felt he really needed a complete change.

'Charlie and Margaret were a perfect match. When they were first together, she was the more serious but had a sense of fun beneath. He joked a lot, but had hidden depths'

But a complete change had already happened, for while he'd been in London, Charlie had met a strikingly attractive and very talented young woman on the same arts course. Her name was Margaret Ingram, and by the time Charlie had decided to leave Manchester she was teaching in the North East. For a while, they conducted a long-distance courtship, he driving up in a Morris 1000 from the North West. Margaret's sister Joan, whose mother was head teacher at Hunstanworth in County Durham, remembers meeting Charlie, who she says was more like a mariner than a teacher. "He had a rolling gait and was immensely cheerful – just like a sailor."

Charlie and Margaret were a perfect match – then, as they always would be. When they were first together, she was the more serious but had a sense of fun beneath. He joked a lot, but had hidden and reflective depths. She had specialised in textiles at Goldsmiths. Their interests and their enthusiasms interleaved as naturally as their respective creations in fabric and glass would over subsequent years.

In 1955 they were married at the register office in Manchester, and moved to Cumbria to settle, first in a windy rainswept cottage near Alston. They later moved to Ring Gate, between Hayton and Castle Carrock, at which point Charlie was happily teaching in the Eden School at Rickerby

Charles Bray

Park, Carlisle. Charlie said Cumbria and Margaret revitalised him.

He was in charge of art and, whatever he passed on to his students, he certainly flourished in the world of art education. In 1962 he left Eden School and took a job at Sunderland Teacher Training College, not long afterwards becoming head of ceramic art at the College of Art – subsequently part of the University of Sunderland.

Charlie and Margaret now had a growing family. In 1957 a son David had been born, followed the next year by another boy, Stephen. Simon came into the world in 1959, and in 1962, the year Charlie moved from Carlisle to Sunderland to work, the family also moved to Farlam, near Brampton, soon after which another boy, Andrew, was born. The house, Prospect House, was to be a place of love and inspiration, a home where Charlie, in work and retirement alike – and Margaret too – were creative.

Sunderland brought out the brilliance in Charlie. A potentially enterprising but neglected institution, its art college gave Charlie the freedom to develop what he realised was his latent passion for glass and ceramics: he himself described his discovery of that passion as "a happy accident". For his students and colleagues, it was an opening of great new possibilities – possibilities that became the reality of Sunderland's pre-eminent role in the field today.

Brian Sefton, who was on the staff of the art college at the time, recalls Charlie's determination to found a glass degree course. He took colleagues to look not only at the Pyrex works – Sunderland's famous home of laboratory and kitchen glassware – but to the glassmakers Hedley Woods, where they used virtually unchanged medieval techniques for producing plate glass. It became apparent that Charlie had an embracing knowledge of the material science behind glassmaking.

But he discovered that there was a shortage of textbooks covering the areas in which he was now so keen to work. So, over the next few years, he wrote them. "The Dictionary of Glass"; "Glassblowing"; and "Ceramics and Glass" became standard works. He had worked out techniques that even the glass industry didn't recognise.

In addition to lobbying and planning successfully for the establishment of the degree course, Charlie was a much-admired teacher. He treated students with respect and concern for their welfare; and he was resourceful to a fault. If the college couldn't afford new equipment, he'd arrive at work with his car laden with components he'd cadged from British Gas.

'The man who had hardly any formal qualifications was eventually awarded an honorary fellowship by the University of Sunderland'

There never would have been a course – or the National Glass Centre in Sunderland – had it not been for Charlie. The man who had hardly any formal qualifications was eventually awarded an honorary fellowship by the university formed from the old Sunderland teacher-training, technical, and art colleges in the 1980s.

During his time there and in his workshop and studio in Farlam, Charlie produced works of glass and ceramic art that found their way into galleries and museums across the world. His work was collected and displayed in the US, the Czech Republic, and at the Turner Glass Museum in Sheffield. Private collectors included Queen Margarethe of Denmark and ex-King Constantine of Greece.

When he was at Goldsmiths, Charlie had visited Vallauris, where Picasso applied his talents to the production of ceramic figures and pottery. There are strong hints in some of Charlie's work of that influence. He was, importantly, a valued member of the Society of Glass Technology.

After Charlie retired from Sunderland, a retirement brought on more by his concern for Margaret's first encounter with cancer than with his desire to give up academic work, he continued to work of art in different media. He worked inside the house too, making tables, designing and constructing doors and door frames – some using ecclesiastical geometry – and staircases. His tongue-and-groove ceiling is masterly.

Then there are the garden figures that blend into the land adjoining the house and studio. Some look as if they have grown out of the rock that lies behind. There are echoes of Ben Nicholson and Miro – but most importantly there is the personality and the originality of Charles Bray. They are unique.

Thinking back to his childhood, Andrew recalls a father who was busy, often away, engaged with one project or another, but who had time to encourage the brothers in whatever they did. All have achieved in their personal and professional lives much that drew Charlie's admiration and approval – even though he'd often pass that admiration on to third parties rather than directly to them. Motoring holidays in Europe, and his building a dinghy to sail on Talkin Tarn, are fondly remembered.

Rita Bray was married to Charlie's cousin George. She has images of the young Charlie coming to see George, ill in Manchester Royal Infirmary, and allowed to stay for only half an hour or so after a journey of three hours from Cumbria.

Talking about Charlie's woodwork and his carving she says it was exceptional and handsome – just like him. And she remembers coming round to Farlam when the three eldest boys were ten or less, seeing them using welding equipment under the careful eyes of their father. He and Margaret often stayed at Rita and George's house in Broadbottom, and the young ones always thought Father Christmas had arrived, whatever month of the year it might be. He always had a twinkle in his eyes.

Mary Craven was married to Vin, the fellow scout. She remembers go-karting competitions, camping trips and voluntary work the scouts did in Salford and beyond. She also – like Rita – recalls the way Charlie let youngsters experiment with glass and other materials.

She tells of the honorary fellowship ceremony at Sunderland, where a grandchild called out audibly as Charlie passed in his robes "There's granddad: why's he wearing a frock?" Mary says he was giving advice only four weeks ago to an A level art student and helped her own grandson gain entrance to art school.

Charlie continued to be his enterprising self long after formal retirement, and when the originally dire prognosis for Margaret back in 1979 proved spurious and she recovered her health, he took a keen interest in her work as an artist and her success – especially the creative brilliance of her quilting. He was close and loving throughout her final illness.

What's left is Charlie's work, his enduring professional reputation, and his family, who resonate with the values and the outlook of the man. His children; his grandchildren Carrianne, Dougie, Lucinda, Thomas, and Joseph; his great grandchildren George and Charlie.

We are, of course, bound to have left out many stories, whole chapters even, of Charlie's life. But we have tried to convey something of the essence of a man who mattered.

The funeral ceremony for Charles Bray was held at Carlisle Crematorium on Tuesday July 31 2012

Peter Johnston

1942-2012

Peter Robin Johnston came into the world in January 1942, the eldest of six children born to Rene and Arthur Johnston. They were Quakers, and Arthur was an engineering draughtsman. Peter's earliest years were spent in the village of Totternhoe in Bedfordshire – not far from Dunstable golf course, which may explain his fascination for a game that would play a very important part in his life.

When he was six, and the family moved to nearby Hertfordshire, there was more of the same. In Gustard Wood, a little hamlet near Wheathampstead, they lived in the gardener's cottage to Delaport House. It was an idyllic place for a boy to grow up: there were streams and spinneys, woodland and hidden trails. It was an age when children were considered safe to be outdoors all day when they weren't at school. Rene, who spent a lot of her time reading, actively encouraged Peter and the younger children to look after themselves.

They lived on the edge of the Mid-Herts golf course, and one day when Peter was about seven he was spotted beside the course by the club pro, Bill Peters. The youngster was wielding a crooked walking stick and using it to hit a tennis ball quite effectively. Bill asked young Peter if he'd like some proper equipment and duly presented the lad with a bag containing four perfectly serviceable clubs. That was the start of Peter's golfing prowess.

A picture of him, aged nine, shows him in confident stance, swinging his club at Gustard Wood and already looking the seasoned professional. His sister Anna Mary recalls hunting in the ponds nearby for golf balls to practise with. They weren't considered to have been dishonestly acquired – just carefully recycled.

Peter's youth was about a lot more than golf, of course. A naturally clever boy, he was even made to stand in a corner at his village school for being – in the teacher's opinion – too bright. He absorbed his mother's love of reading and devoured everything he could get his hands on; he took an interest in the wider world around him; at age 11 he won a place at St Alban's Grammar – known for its exceptional academic standards. Stephen Hawking was one of Peter's classmates.

But as well as his academic achievements – testimony of which was his eventual admission to Queen's College, Cambridge – Peter's passion and proficiency for golf flourished. Anna Mary remembers that throughout his teenage years the house was increasingly adorned with golfing trophies won by her talented older brother. Almost as a sideline, he was also excelling at rugby and proving an all-round cricketer.

Peter Johnston

At Cambridge, Peter read history for two years then decided he wanted to switch to law. He did – and graduated in just one year. It was positive proof of those qualities by which he was to be known: determination, clear-thinking focus, capability. And through it all ran not only the threads of his sporting, mainly golfing, inclinations, but also his developing love and knowledge of music and literature.

All of these were interests shared with Annabel Page when she met Peter at Cambridge. She was a postgraduate student doing experimental psychology and he was in that finals year when he had swapped history for law. They had both set themselves punishing work timetables, they shared a space with a gas fire to keep them warm in what was one of the coldest winters on record, and they were, quite simply, very good student friends.

Romance was not at this juncture any part of their life together, but golf was. Annabel was a very good player and – in the chauvinistic world they then inhabited – was "allowed" to play at Peter's club in Cambridge, which drew them close together; but they were apart again after Peter took a position as articled clerk to a firm of solicitors in London, where he was, in Annabel's words "little more than a skivvy" to the partners.

'A naturally clever boy, Peter was made to stand in a corner at his village school for being – in the teacher's opinion – too bright'

She had gone to work in Norwich, which is where, to cut a longer story short, they eventually married and settled. Peter had become a solicitor there after serving his articles: he was able to draw on valuable experience he'd had during university years working with the United Nations Association on building projects for a post office in Austria; for Sainsbury's; and as a teacher briefly in Hamond's Grammar School in Swaffham.

In 1971, while they were living in Norwich, Peter and Annabel had a son Miles. He remembers from his early years a father who was loving and patient, who taught him to play golf and table tennis, who was always a champion of anyone or any group who were in need. Miles recalls visiting his dad in his office in town in the wonderfully-named Tombland Alley. He also remembers how his father was considerate, treating his son as an equal and with respect.

While they lived in Norfolk (improbably, given the topography of that county) Peter developed an interest in mountaineering and also, somewhat esoterically, caving. It was a long distance from anywhere that satisfied either of those enthusiasms, but with friends he travelled to and became familiar with the hills and fells of Derbyshire, then Scotland and the Lake District.

One of the friends he made at that time was John Crawford. His widow, Judith, describes the strength of fellow-feeling the two men developed through their love of golfing but also as hiking companions. Peter and Miles visited them often, and it was with the Crawfords that Peter first walked and climbed in the Peak District. Judith recalls with some amazement how Peter was able to play golf effortlessly and superbly well even after not having lifted a club for three or four years.

Peter and the Crawfords walked in all weathers and in many locations, shared interests in literature and music and especially in wine and good food. He visited often when the Crawfords moved to Nottingham. Judith couldn't be with us today but came to see him – in the hospice – two weeks or so ago, and notes that "there was laughter as well as some tears."

Over the next few years, during which he established his own successful law practice in Norwich, Peter continued to expand such interests. Sadly, but slowly and amicably, those interests diverged from Annabel's, and they gradually drifted apart.

After a long-drawn-out, but never disagreeable, parting of the ways, the two divorced in 1986. It was the end of Peter's marriage but prefaced the beginning of his new life in Cumbria, to which he moved in 1989. He was by now a very experienced lawyer, having specialised in wills, probate, and tax planning. Moving first to Curthwaite, he had no difficulty in finding similar work with a Carlisle law firm, Bendles.

Soon Peter joined Beaty & Co in Wigton, a law firm with whom he was to be a partner for more than 20 years – and for which he was still a consultant in recent months. Beaty's John Hawkes, says they "hit it off" immediately when they first met. It was a partnership with never a cross word, Peter was a man of unimpeachable integrity and took on all the big, complex, difficult cases – and did them brilliantly.

According to John, clients from all over the country recognised his focused honesty and his unconditional attention to detail. He was – and others say this too – a worrier, but, as his son Miles observes, it was his way to ponder a problem for ages and then emerge with an answer that was practically and ethically the right one. John remembers also the lighter touches, like Peter's love of Red Bush tea taken in a Willow Pattern cup.

When John Hawkes was ill, diagnosed with cancer in 2010, Peter held the Beaty fort superbly, only to discover shortly after John's return, that he was suffering from the same disease though of a more serious nature. But this is to skip past far more important events in Peter's life which happened after he came to live in Cumbria.

The first is that he met George and Audrey Heslop who were neighbours when Peter moved in 1989 to Old Crown Cottage at Hesket Newmarket. They became the firmest of friends, a friendship eventually transformed into something more in 2009, when, appropriately on St Audrey's Day – October 17 – Peter and Audrey, by then long widowed, were married. Peter had asked her four times to marry him and eventually said "I'm not going to ask you again." He didn't have to. By then he had established not only a life in Cumbria but as a regular visitor to Scotland.

'Peter had asked Audrey four times to marry him and eventually said "I'm not going to ask you again." He didn't have to'

Nick Gardner and his wife Janet had a cottage to let near Gairloch, not far from their home in Wester Ross. Peter answered an ad in 1995 and became a regular visitor - twice a year for ten years - and a very close friend, with the cottage a glorious base for walking and climbing. There are many pictures of Peter, his face all smiles, on peaks like An Teallach, which involved a 12-hour ascent.

He had first come with a group from Norwich and soon Nick and Janet got to know him through walking and climbing together – learned about and shared his enthusiasms for music, cricket, and golf and became acquainted with the changes happening in his professional and personal life. They met him and Audrey together for the first time there in 2004. He was, says Janet, so calm, so kind, so full of gentleness.

Frankie Hart was a close friend of Peter's and deeply involved, like her late husband Sir David, in education. It was Frankie who sold Old Crown Cottage to Peter when he first came to Hesket Newmarket, and Peter was to become a fellow governor of Fell View Primary School in Caldbeck. Frankie writes of this time:

"Peter was successively vice-chairman and treasurer until he left the school governing body in 1997 at the same time as I retired. As well as championing the pure academic side of education, he was passionate about education in its wider sense encompassing the arts, music, the outdoors and sports. He felt that a good school should not just teach but inspire and enthuse children to learn.

"Once, he learned that the school budget was to be so seriously cut back that the governing body decided the only way forward was to make the part-time music teacher redundant. Our music teacher was excellent and much-loved by the pupils. Peter took the matter into his own hands by raising several thousand pounds, working hard to get people up and down the land to sponsor him to climb Britain's three highest peaks within 24 hours.

"Peter set off with two friends and succeeded with less than half an hour to spare. A fantastic achievement! He enabled specialist music teaching to continue. The music teacher was in tears with gratitude and the staff and children were cheering Peter loudly.

"Peter spent hours each month checking the school accounts. He was a brilliant treasurer and nothing missed his fine attention to detail. He once asked me as head teacher about £100 spent on miscellaneous staff expenses. I told him the money was for wine for the staff to celebrate the end of term. Peter was not amused and was relieved when I explained I was only teasing and the money was really for advertising in the *Times Educational Supplement* for a new infant teacher.

"I knew him as a man who was loyal, sensitive, deep-thinking, caring, trustworthy, helpful, kind, intelligent, thoughtful and who was so very talented as a lawyer, sportsman, climber, gardener, geologist, mountaineer, food and wine connoisseur.

"Peter was one of the very best friends I ever had. He was in every sense an extraordinary man and will be sorely missed. He will always have a large place in my heart."

Audrey has written movingly of her time with Peter and of the profound love and respect they had for one another. He was, she says, a 'people's person' – just as golf is 'the people's game.' A man so clever and intelligent but one whose regard was the same for the dustman as for the most eminent individual he'd ever met. And he was interested in everything – philosophy, music, sport, the arts, gardening. His greatest personal quality was his true friendship to so many – a gentle man who was a gentleman.

Audrey talks of the way he dealt with his illness – total acceptance from the beginning and never the words 'Why me?' His principles and his attitude to life were unchanged by his failing health – and his last words to his nurses were 'Thank you, thank you, thank you.'

As Audrey says, his love for his family, for Miles and Naty, for the grandchildren Alex and Elliott, 'and of course me!' drove and inspired him.

Peter would have appreciated Audrey's observation that Stephen Hawking, the former classmate, introducing the London Paralympics, enjoined his audience to "Look at the stars and not down at your feet. Be curious." That was certainly Peter's philosophy too. Audrey ends with these wonderfully optimistic words:

"There was his love of animals: he was on the same wavelength as the cats, and they knew: the dog Poppy too, who was with him when he passed away so peacefully. I thought the swallows and house martins had left the other week, but they must have been on a training flight during the bad weather and are now here in force, saying goodbye to the house and their nests. They will take Peter's spirit with them . . . and return next year."

In all that we have heard, what emerges is that Peter Johnston retained and honed the values with which he started in life – the values of a Quaker family and an era and a place long gone but in which honour and attainment, and an abiding interest in one's environment, directed everything he did.

The funeral ceremony for Peter Johnston was held at Carlisle Crematorium on Monday September 10 2012

Life has its own meaning

Introducing a funeral ceremony at Hexham in 2004 Ian said: "Humanism is a philosophy based upon understanding, compassion, tolerance, reason and, above all, a sense of the basic goodness and dignity of human kind and the Humanist perception that life has meaning without there being any need for supernatural explanation."

Philosophical reinforcements, as needed, tend to come from great twentieth-century thinkers like Bertrand Russell and Herbert Read.

Russell compared life to water running from mountain source to sea, the passionate early stream, the quieter mid-life river and the final painless merger with the ocean.

Read's analogy is that of the tree of life: the human race is its trunk and branches; individuals, as leaves, get their sap and collective consciousness from the tree; and when leaves wither and die they help to nourish forthcoming generations.

Ceremonies celebrate life, a life, but they also offer comfort to those who remain. In this area, verse has the ability to explore the unknown and somehow relate us to it intimately as individuals.

For the eight lives whose stories have been told here, Ian called on, amongst others, Shakespeare in The Tempest ("We are such stuff as dreams are made of"), Samuel Butler ("I fall asleep in the full and certain hope, That my slumber shall not be broken"), Sylvia Plath ("To forget time, to forgive the world, to be at peace"), Pam Ayres ("Don't lay me in some gloomy churchyard shrouded by a wall...Lay me in some leafy loam...") and of course Joyce Grenfell ("If I should go before the rest of you, Break not a flower nor inscribe a stone... Parting is hell, but life goes on").

None of these carry Humanist copyright. They are all incorporated without issue in religious ceremonies these days, along with music of whatever brand. But Humanists return to the individual, the singular life that is being remembered, and his or her circle of family and friends. As Ian put it only last year:

"There's an enduring spirit that springs from all we do or say during our lives. Nothing of us that matters is ever really lost – and that continuity far outlasts the brief span of time we spend on this small planet. Indeed the only promise of immortality we have is what lies in the minds and memories of those who have known us."

Duke elegy

by Ian Breach

Edward Kennedy "Duke" Ellington, who died yesterday, was the first and last man to encompass the whole wisdom of an era of jazz. He changed and permanently influenced the development of his entire field. With a few exceptions, no other jazz musician could compare in the range, the quality, the volume and the sheer inventiveness of Ellington.

Born in 1899 and a professional pianist by his late teens, he made his first record in 1924 and his last not many weeks ago. Between them he must have put close on 5,000 titles on disc, tape and film – for there are countless private and unissued recordings of his work.

His career began as a "stride" pianist – a keyboard fashion that explains itself. From there, he evolved a way of playing which could be florid at one end of the scale or economic to the point of austerity, but which was unmistakably his own: concise but warm, logical but surprising, catchy but immensely clever. So easy when it is done but so difficult to achieve, he made all his music, with one or two special exceptions, simple without being undemanding.

In applying this approach to the band he kept together for well over 40 years, he succeeded in bringing off a paradox in the extempore world of jazz, disciplining though never stifling the talents of an army of effervescent soloists. Many of these were geniuses in their own right, with so many ideas that it often seemed impossible to get them through one instrument in conventional time and space. Ellington was the bandleader who had what it took to marshal the resources.

Not surprisingly, the repertoire of the orchestra was usually based on works written by Ellington or in collaboration with his close friend and arranger, Billy Strayhorn, who died seven years ago: works like "Mood Indigo", "Satin Doll", "Things Ain't What They Used To Be", and "Take the 'A' Train". There were also the suites and specially written scores which span 50 years and which were heard live in places as far apart as Kalamazoo and Coventry Cathedral.

But Ellington was alive and alert to everyone else's music. In the thirties and forties he was listening to and developing from the music of the stage shows. In 1960 he went back to Tchaikovsky for inspiration: later still he adapted from the best of the Beatles – a double payment of musical compliments.

There was some mild Uncle Tom-ism in Ellington. Not so much as in Louis Armstrong, perhaps, but he nevertheless walked on a lot of red carpets and shook a good many plump white hands that no modern black

American musician would want to know about. It is sad – and maybe one of the reasons why – most people have heard of him and not of them.

At least it can be said that he accepted all the worship, the honour and the trappings of being a master with great dignity and not a little humour. He is unlikely to be mourned in the real sense of the word. He will be celebrated – and his influence will last for ages.

Reprinted from the Guardian, Saturday May 25 1974

Picture captions

6 Top : Ian with his father before Eric left for war service in the Far East during 1941; bottom left: Doris Breach, Ian's mother 7 Ian passed his 11+ but became the "class clown and wastrel" at grammar school 10 Ian as an apprentice Merchant Navy engineer on board the Zenetia 11 Ian and Jacky on their wedding day, London, 1961 13 Ian when Guardian technology correspondent 14 Ian poses as Ian Carr, Manchester, mid-1960s 15 Breach family, Manchester, 1966: Ian, his father Eric, Jacky and Emmie. Picture by Patrick Swithenbank 23 Ian on Bideford beach, Devon, when making the BBC-tv film Tarka's Troubled Water. Picture by John Hayes Fisher 27 Ian and Wendy Breach at their wedding celebration, Loweswater, December 2007. 31 Mollie Pearson Abbott as a senior student 37 Mollie greeting the Duke of Edinburgh at a Dunfermline College graduation ceremony, 1970s 41 Julie Broadhurst on her allotment, 2004 49 Karen Foulds, August 2008 57 Leslie Halliman in 2009 65 Deborah Sue Godsey with her nieces Heidi, Monica and Andrea at St Andrews, October 2000 71 Hetty Baron-Thieme as a young woman 79 Charles Bray 83 Charlie in his studio at Farlam 87 Peter Johnston hiking in Scotland
Inside back cover Ian in Wales, July 2012
Back cover Robert Waterhouse and Ian Breach, Nice, 2001

Excerpts from Ian's funeral

Humanism was a big part of Ian's philosophy, the belief that we get one chance at life and that this existence on earth is the one that should engage our energies and ambitions, so this ceremony has celebrated Ian's life as well as acknowledging your loss and grief. It has been an occasion for you to express your gratitude for all that you shared and enjoyed with Ian – the essence of what made him the man for whom you cared.

Grief can be a lonely experience but we are here today to share those feelings of loss and pain with Ian's wife Wendy, his daughter Emmie and her husband Guy, and their children Maisie, Rosa, Stella and Theo. Ian's oldest grandchild, Oskar, is also here today with his partner Sophie, as are Wendy's children, Ian's step-children, Gillian, Emily, Christine and Michael.

Memories of Ian will endure, for, whatever relationship you may have had with him, the rewards of having had that relationship will never be lost.

At the graveside:

We now come to the conclusion of this ceremony for Ian who will be part of this place for all time. Through the freshness of successive springs, the warmth of summer, and the mists of autumn, and the bitter cold of winter he will always be at peace.

We commit Ian's body to the natural safety of the earth, which sustains and regenerates all life. We dedicate this simple plot to every good and precious memory associated with him. The occasion may cause us to reflect on the continuity of all life: nothing of us, except our conscious being, is indestructible, and interment reunites us in a profound way with the natural universe.

After burial:

In a spirit of love, let us remember Ian's life and the part you played in it. And, thinking of him, go peacefully to celebrate that life together.

Ian's funeral ceremony was held at St Andrew's Chapel and Woodland Burial Ground, Hexham, conducted by Humanist celebrant Jan Dunckley, on Monday February 4 2013